THE HEART AND SOUL

OF

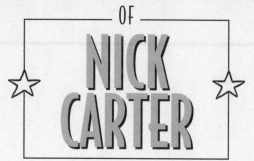

NICK CARTER

THE HEART AND SOUL

OF

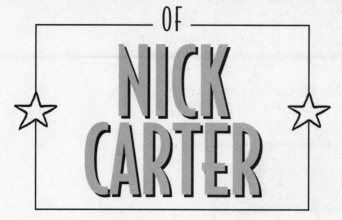

NICK CARTER

Secrets Only a Mother Knows

by JANE CARTER

AN ONYX BOOK

ONYX
Published by the Penguin Group
Penguin Putnam Inc., 375 Hudson Street,
New York, New York 10014, U.S.A.
Penguin Books Ltd, 27 Wrights Lane,
London W8 5TZ, England
Penguin Books Australia Ltd,
Ringwood, Victoria, Australia
Penguin Books Canada Ltd, 10 Alcorn Avenue,
Toronto, Ontario, Canada M4V 3B2
Penguin Books (N.Z.) Ltd, 182–190 Wairau Road,
Auckland 10, New Zealand

Penguin Books Ltd, Registered Offices:
Harmondsworth, Middlesex, England

First published by Onyx, an imprint of Dutton NAL,
a member of Penguin Putnam Inc.

First Printing, December 1998
10 9 8 7 6 5 4 3

To Nick,
and for young people all over the world . . .
for those, even the wounded ones,
who have the strength to love life.

ACKNOWLEDGMENTS

First of all, I wish to thank my dad, Douglas Spaulding, who encouraged me to write this book. His love has always carried the message "You can do it!" My father retyped my handwritten narrative at the beginning. Meanwhile, he researched all the details of our family tree.

I'd like to thank Margaret Sagarese, who helped me reach the finish line with my manuscript, turning my dream for this book into a reality. Thanks, too, to her daughter, Skyler, for inspiration.

I send my gratitude to Denise Marcil, my literary agent, who believed I should tell my story about raising Nick my way. Denise didn't give up until we found a publisher who agreed.

Thanks to Carolyn Nichols at New American Library, who put my book on the right track as well as the fast track, and to all those at NAL who worked extra-hard and extra-quickly on the project.

Sometimes I forget to express this, but I want to officially recognize the love and support of my husband, Bob, and all my children—BJ, Leslie, Angel, Aaron, and Nick. This is Nick's story, because he was the first of my children to inspire me. I want the rest of you to know that I will help you write your special lifescripts, too.

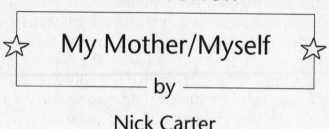

My Mother/Myself

by

Nick Carter

Did I sense that my destiny was different from other kids when I was younger? Good question.

Before the age of eight or nine, I really didn't know what my destiny was. How could I? I just went to school and lived the kind of normal, everyday life that boys that age live—except that I loved music, listening to it and making it, particularly by singing.

The turning point was one day when I serenaded my mom from a tree stump. (She'll tell you all about it.) My mom believed in me. I wish every child could have a mother or a father who cares enough to spot his talent and help him develop it the way mine did.

I really didn't know where my talent would lead me at first. When I started to follow the music inside me, I took vocal lessons, but since I wasn't sure exactly what I wanted to do, I tried not only singing, but also acting.

My mother chauffeured me up and down from Tampa to Orlando, from Tampa to St. Petersburg, back and forth, more times than I can tell you. Often my chances of landing a part were less than slim. Mom agreed to let me try anyway. She spent money on traveling, on lessons, when our family didn't have extra. Our family business supported us for the basics. Our clothes and our food were taken care of, but there wasn't much left after that. Any extra money was almost always spent on me and my dream of becoming an entertainer.

When I became discouraged, Mom used to quietly ask me, "Nick, are you sure you want to do this?" Although it was hard work for a kid, I knew in my heart I did, so I always told her, "Yes."

When you are ten or eleven or twelve, you may know what you want to do. You may know where you want to go, but without someone to help you get there, you're stuck. I see many young people who don't do anything. They have no dreams. I had a dream and a mother who believed in me. I am living proof that with a belief in yourself and an adult to help, the sky's the limit.

My mom doesn't know this because I've never told her, but even though I was young, I realized what sacrifices she was making for me. I saw my mom and dad do without, so that there would be traveling money, money for vocal lessons, money for dance lessons. I wanted the day to come—someday— when I could make things better for them.

As you know, it has all worked out for the best. My mom has been very influential in my success. And so has my dad. I love my whole family—but I not only love, I *like* my parents and I'm very grateful to them, especially my mom. Without them, I might not have achieved my dream so young. Maybe I would have achieved it when I was much older. Nick Carter, rising thirty-year-old star? I don't think so.

I could go out to a mall, and purchase something to show my gratitude to my parents. But what amount do you spend to say thank you for faith, hope, and love—the things my mom gave me? No fancy car or piece of jewelry compares. So Mom, what I want you to know is that your love nourished me, your faith in me helped me focus—and my hope and yours paved my way. That's what I want you to know, from my heart to your heart.

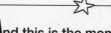

And this is the moment when I want to thank my very first fan . . . Mom.

I am very grateful to be in this position. I want to thank all my fans.

Thank you.

Love,

Nick

Dreaming—The Carter Family Way

When I decided to take this written walk down memory lane, I wanted not only to recount the events of the early years in Nick's and my journey from obscurity to worldwide fame, but also to recapture the emotion that fueled us. And so, to start, I traveled north to my father's house in upstate New York where he kept a very special box, a cardboard treasure chest.

As proud mothers do, I saved everything— playbills and flyers from every event Nick participated in: an elementary school play, talent shows, community theater productions, home videos, and any footage for which I could get copies of his performances.

I couldn't wait to open that box, because I felt certain that once I held Nick's scuffed tap shoes in my hands, and clapped them together, that click would help me remember vivid details to put down on paper. If I looked into Nick's eyes, staring back at me from an old black-and-white glossy, his sparkle could illuminate our yesterdays. I wanted the floodgates of my memory to swing open so readers could relive Nick's childhood with me, feel the high hopes as passionately as we did.

Nick and I were forever running to talent shows and contests—as well as audition after audition—trying to get one big break. Every time we went off to that new show, that first contest, that next competition, we talked optimistically and enthusiastically.

Solemnly and hopefully, one of us always whispered, "This might be the one!" A question mark and an exclamation point, a wish and a prayer, a conviction and a drive—all these nestled and jockeyed within our mantra. We spoke the words out loud as if doing so had the power to make it real for Nick this time. Even our silences echoed with this wish to make it so.

At the beginning we had each other and the dream. We imagined meeting some big shot with admiration lilting in his voice, money bulging out of his pockets, and love beating in his heart. The mogul would walk up and say, "Hey, kid, you're great! Here's a contract. Here's a pile of money. I'm going to make you a big star." It didn't happen that way, of course, but we logged a lot of time hoping. It was Nick and me against the world, against the odds.

As I sat with this box on my lap, my cardboard

cache didn't disappoint me. Unfolding and sorting through the keepsakes and remnants, all of my recollections welled up. Seeing the photographs and touching the past, I felt as though I was being overwhelmed with the sights and sounds of Nick's childhood. As I ran my fingers over the laminated first resume I typed up when Nick was just ten, then the shiny, white satin fringe of his Elvis costume, Nick shimmered and shimmied right before my eyes. In an instant, I became intoxicated with familiar feelings: delight, nervous butterflies, nervous tension. I felt yesterday's adrenaline pumping Nick up for a contest. I tasted and savored sweet rushes of triumph. And I felt again anxiety interlaced with hope as we faced challenges and overcame obstacles. These were the sensations that Nick and I, united against whatever forces tried to keep us from reaching his dream, lived and breathed.

Of all the images of superstar Nick Carter that people have seen, there is *one* that no one but Nick and I and members of the family know about. You won't see it among the glossy close-ups published in *BOP!*, *BB*, *Superteen*, *Teen Beat*, *All Stars*, *Faces in Pop*, *Teen Machine*, or *Starz*. You won't be able to download it from the frontiers of cyberspace. No, this picture of Nick is different. It is a one-of-a-kind. It's the first in a family archive of Nick Carter that you will be treated to within the pages of this book.

For me, it is the first image ever of Nick. The credit for capturing this premier glimpse of Nick does not belong to European paparazzi. A teenage girl is responsible for this first, never-before-seen rendering of Nick.

Once upon a time a fifteen-year-old girl stood at an easel with a paint brush in one hand. A palette splotched with gobs of acrylic paints rested in the other. The young adolescent artist was me. I painted a young boy with elegantly clean facial features and a dazzling crown of blond hair. I colored my six-year-old all-American boy with blue jeans and a plaid shirt. I angled him in a kneeling pose, holding a large glass jar that contained monarch butterflies.

At the time I couldn't tell you why I painted that particular portrait. I thought it was about me. As things turned out, it is all about Nick.

I believed I painted it because I loved playing tag with butterflies as a child. In September, monarch butterflies migrate south to warmer weather and dine on full-blooming red monarda flowers. I loved catching one of these butterflies, holding it captive if only for a day. I'd feed my fluttering prisoner a carefully blended potion of sugar and water. I promised to set my guest free soon, and I always kept my promise.

Wherever I went, my work of art went along with me in my suitcase. When I left home to get married, it was in my wedding chest. It hangs today in our home in Florida.

When I see it now, it's both obvious and eerie. The boy in the acrylic painting bears an uncanny resemblance to Nick! The look-alike on bended knee peering through the glass at butterflies foreshadowed a young boy who would one day capture this beautiful dream. (And he *did* struggle with stage fright, the butterflies-in-the-stomach species.) Only now do I understand why I protected it with a passion.

Anyone who ever looked at my painting thought surely that I deliberately painted Nick. When I tell them that I did the portrait almost six years before his birth, people have the same startled reaction. No, this isn't the *X-Files*. I am not a clairvoyant.

I'm telling you about this painting because I think it illustrates, oddly enough, the future that my son would encounter. As I brushed those strokes onto canvas I believe I was preparing myself for this handsome and special blond boy that I would raise. He would grow up crystallizing a kind of star quality, transforming from boy to teen, from a moth to a dazzler. This boy wanted to fly, to sing his way into the stratosphere.

As his mother I would leave behind my butterfly-catching memories and take up helping my son on his quest to catch a more elusive quarry . . . stardom.

Yes, before Nick was even born, before I ever became his mother, the vision of him already existed clearly in my mind, although when I first held Nick and nurtured him I didn't know the particulars of his destiny.

Being in Tune with Nick

To really provide you with the key to understanding Nick, and how everything that happened to him fell into place, I think it's important to explain who I am, and I will do that along the way. To give you the whole story about Nick's beginnings, you'll meet Nick's father, Bob, on these pages. Nick grew up in a wild bunch of sorts with siblings, even if he was, from day one, the leader of the pack. Nick has a brother and three spirited sisters. The oldest is Bobbie Jean, but we call her "BJ." BJ, who is sixteen now, has been known to tell her big brother on more than one occasion, "You are not king around here, your costume doesn't work on us!" Leslie is twelve, the middle child. You know Aaron, who is ten, but less about Angel, who is Aaron's twin.

In order to truly understand the heart, the mind, the thinking and the soul of Nick, you have to get inside the Carter family and our philosophy, too. Nick was encouraged to be his true self and to express his natural talents. Nick's father and I created the cocoon where Nick developed his confidence. When the glimmer of a dream began forming, Nick got all the help he needed from me and the rest of his family to grow that dream.

How did we as parents do that? I had a set of beliefs about children, about parents, and about life. I learned much of this at my own father's knee.

Nick's Dream Workbook

LESSON #1   The Dream Scheme

I believe that *each person born into this world comes with a special and unique talent.* Nick grew up learning to look at all people this way.

According to our Carter family code, every child is a person, not a thing, with a purpose and a goal. As Nick's mother, I felt it to be my sacred commitment to help my son find out who he was and help him get in touch with his purpose. The question that mattered most to me was, What is Nick's special gift?

With some children, it's obvious. My brothers excelled in sports and academics. With other boys and girls, there is no particular single interest. In that case, the parents' job is to be patient. A child who can't find a defining talent should experiment and try different things until something catches his or her imagination.

Virtually from the beginning of his life, Nick gravitated—and gyrated even in his diapers—to music. He had a fascination for rhythm.

> With Nick we didn't have to stumble through a maze or solve a mystery to discover his talent and passion for performing.

As his little personality formed, Nick's musical gift revealed itself. When I put my son to the "what made him happiest" test, Nick knew—even in his earliest years. He displayed the most pure, unbridled joy when he was singing, playing entertainer, and performing in one mischievous way or another.

Nick Carter hears music in his head. He listens and writes it into songs. At this moment he is busy writing some songs for Aaron's next album. Melodies always floated around in Nick's head. When he was a child he often didn't know what to do with the music inside him, but as he grew he found ways to let it all come out. Music is at the very core of Nick's being . . . at the very heart and soul of him.

LESSON #2   The Dream Team

I believe *it is a parent's responsibility to nurture the talent or passion* that a child possesses. What other job could be more important?

When I recognized Nick's talent, when he told me first with his enthusiasm and then with words that he wanted to become a musical performer, I did exactly what I knew needed to be done to help. I became his supporter, his mentor, and his loving guide. I worked on Nick and with Nick so that he could become who he truly wanted to be. Nick was determined to grow into his best self as a singer, a dancer, and as an entertainer.

My experiences as a child, and then as Nick's mother, probably contributed to how Nick feels about music and the arts. When becoming a singing sensation monopolized his imagination, I felt very in sync with that ambition. I loved music myself at an early age. I remember my parents' stereo blasting with the Beatles singing "Sergeant Pepper's Lonely Hearts Club Band" or songs off the famous *White Album.* I danced and sang to those classic '60s lyrics before I had any idea of what I was singing about. I had the music gene, if not the desire to perform in front of others. I wholeheartedly endorsed Nick's going further with his musical game plan.

LESSON #3   Dream Weaving

Nick's road to success is so clear to me now as I look back at his early years. But back at the beginning, when Nick was my baby, nothing was clear. I just started out loving him.

Both my son and I profited from this way of looking at children. We were lucky that I believed (and
still do) that a mother's job was to tune in to her
child. Children are not born merely to obey parents.
*Children are born to obey a larger order or calling, which
is to be true to themselves, to become who they are meant
to be.* My job was to help Nick find his voice, then
find a way for the rest of the world to hear the beauty
of his song.

Everything I know now about good parenting is
clearer. Just like all children can teach their parents,
Nick taught me a thing or two about parenting. He
showed me that with the right amount of love, free-
dom, and encouragement, anything is possible. I told
him as much over the years and he gave it right back
to me.

LESSON #4   There Is No Such Thing as an Impossible Dream

Nick would not be where he is today if not for the
next important rule in the family philosophy: *dare to
dream.* Dreaming is, always has been, the family way
of doing things. If you don't dream it, then you can't
make a dream come true.

I believe, and I taught Nick that there is no such
thing as an "impossible" dream. Dreams are not like
instant cocoa, though. They take time. They need
perseverance. So to help, I have always been fond of
collecting sayings and slogans about dreams. When
you hit a discouraging patch, and your dream really
does seem impossible, I taught Nick to repeat pro-

dream, positive messages to himself. My conversations with Nick over the years always had these two words in them: "Be positive." In the Carter household, my children throw out the words "I can't," substituting "I can."

"You must make of life a dream, and of a dream . . . a reality." I love that quote. I wish I'd written it, but actually it was Madame Curie, the famous scientist, who did.

I set a good example as a dreamer. I don't mean that I wanted to become a singing sensation. My dreams were basic when Nick was a child. I wanted to survive and create a better life for Nick. Constructing a dream of a better life, and setting about to find a way to make it happen, was the way I have lived my life. Sometimes I've had to put my dreams up on a shelf, go back to square one, and start brain-storming all over again. Growing up with Bob and me, Nick was bound to catch our dreaming fever.

LESSON #5   Be a Determined Dreamer

A dreamer never gives up. Dreaming is a big part of who I am. I cultivated that vision in Nick, too. He saw me and Bob building our dreams. In a child's way he realized that dreams are works in progress. . . .

LESSON #6   Be an Active Dreamer, Not a Passive Dreamer

Dreams have to be put into action. Nick and I are and always have been "experienced dreamers." I set the standard that if you have a dream you must do more than flex the wish bone. It is absolutely vital to go to the next level . . . to follow through. After all, the world is full of dreamers with beautiful dreams. Since this is true, why aren't there more happy endings?

Too often people fail to combine dreaming with doing. I've always made it a conscious choice to be sure to include that subsequent action. I take Aristotle at his word when he says, "The center of life is action."

LESSON #7   Mow Down Any Obstacles to Your Dream

If you encounter obstacles, go around, over, or through them! We used every extra ounce of energy and every extra dollar to pursue Nick's dream. We didn't make excuses, such as "We can't do this or that because we don't have the money." We found the money. I did fancy accounting and juggled the family budget.

The same goes for time. I had my regular work at our family business, a family to take care of, and a marriage. But I always made the time. Occasionally, the other members of our family, Nick's sisters and brother, complained that Nick got a great deal more attention than anyone else. I couldn't argue because that was true. I tried to make my other children feel special in other ways, to the best of my ability.

My commitment renewed itself each time I saw how excited Nick was when he performed, not to mention how much excitement he always generated in his audience.

LESSON #8 Turn Yourself into a Dream Showcase

You have to take advantage of opportunities.
Nick and I agreed that Nick could make it happen, if only he could be seen by the right person. He wanted to stay out there in the spotlight, even though our local spotlight wasn't bright by Hollywood or Broadway standards. He had to be in the right place at the right time. Since we couldn't know where that was or exactly what time was right, we went after as many opportunities as possible. You never knew who was watching. Nick set the agenda; I drove the car . . . and drove . . . and drove.

LESSON #9 Dreams Don't Die

I taught Nick that you can never give up on yourself. When you hear the word "dream" and imagine all the details of the fantasy life that Nick lives now, it sounds magical. Alas, there is a flip side to this dreaming business. The dark side is having to withstand the negatives of dream-weaving. Hand in hand with it go disappointment, discouragement, pain and hurt. Adversity, as my father calls it. "Sweet are the uses of adversity," he was fond of saying.

LESSON #10 Dream Power

I've drummed it into Nick's head his whole life that when a person becomes successful, then it is time to give something back. *Spread the value of dreaming and believing in yourself.*

Was my Nick a dreamer? Absolutely. Was I? Guilty! My dreaming and dreams affected Nick, who created his own unique versions. For a boy whose dream always seemed bigger than he was when he first envisioned it, stardom doesn't get any more satisfying or fulfilling than it does for Nick.

The Nick Carter Dream Instruction Guide

D The D in dream is definitely for drive.

R The R is to stay real and be relentless when your dream seems as if it's never going to materialize.

E The E is for ecstasy. You have to love doing what you dream of.

A The A is for ambition. As long as you love what you do, the hard work will be worth it.

M The M is for the mission. You have to take one day at a time because achieving a dream takes time. But you have time . . . a lifetime to make your mark.

2

☆ Born to Rock ☆

The newspaper clipping of Nick Carter's birth announcement is a little yellowed now.

> CARTER—To Robert and Jane Spaulding Carter of
> R.D. 2, Mayville, in WCA Hospital, January 28, 1980,
> a son.

As a new mother reading Nick's birth announcement in our local paper, I never even dreamed that this was only the first of the thousands of times I would see his name in print. When I opened cards from my relatives and friends that said, "Congratulations on the birth of your son!", I never even imagined that a little over a decade later birthday cards would come tumbling, pouring, flooding through the mail to Nick from fans all over the world.

And I, too, am always surprised and touched to be remembered by hundreds upon hundreds of fans on

Nick's birthday and on Mother's Day. "Thank you so much, Mrs. Carter, for bringing Nick into the world" is the way that many of those cards and letters begin. I've also received moving notes from mothers of Nick's fans. Here's one dated January 28, 1998:

Dear Jane,

I took my 13-year-old to a Backstreet Boys concert last night in Albany because she is hopelessly in love with your son, Nick. We drove 3 hours to get there. (Don't tell, but it was on a school night, too.) The last time I went to a rock concert was so long ago I can't even tell you who I saw.

This was my daughter's first concert. We stood chilled to the bone outside the Palace Theater in Albany, in the thick of a wraparound crowd of thrilled (and shrill!) teenyboppers. When the doors opened, I feared we'd get trampled getting to our seats.

I wasn't expecting to enjoy the show much, although I like listening to Nick's music. Lo and behold, I got caught up in all the energy and excitement. My daughter squealed, and screamed. Clearly Nick sent her straight to heaven.

During intermission she looked at me and said, "Thanks, Mom."

People say raising teenagers is no fun. Well, they are wrong! Last night I shared a "first" with my daughter. It was an evening we both will never forget.

I couldn't let the emotional moment go without thanking you from one mother to another mother.

Whenever January 28 rolls around, I reminisce about the circumstances surrounding Nick's birth. I'm sure that every mother has a special story to tell. All mothers remember the day their child came into their lives, and having a healthy baby has to be one of the happiest days in a woman's life. I'll never forget when the doctor put Nick into my arms, or the events leading up to it.

Nick's father, Robert Gene Carter, whom we call Bob, and I got married young. I met Bob accidentally.

I was working as a waitress, and the car I drove was not in very good condition. When it broke down, I was in a fix: I knew I had to get to work no matter what, car or no car. I didn't want to lose my job. So I did what a lot of impulsive teenagers did back then. I decided to hitchhike to my job, so I walked to the road and stuck out my thumb. (Now, of course, we know that hitchhiking is foolhardy. It's playing Russian roulette with serial killers, who have been known to cruise the highways looking for lone women just like me that day.)

I felt too nervous about getting fired to think straight about the danger of what I was doing. Bob saw me, slowed down, and picked me up. The first words out of his mouth were both charming and scolding, "You shouldn't be hitchhiking!"

At the time, Bob drove a truck on long-distance runs. He worked for a company based in Erie, Pennsylvania, called Hammermill Papers. His father, Charles, who is nicknamed Chuck, also drove for that company, and Bob and his father were often paired as a driving team. It's a good thing they weren't together that day, because Bob might not have slowed down to check me out and give me a lift.

Bob's courtly gesture and his offer to drive me to work didn't win my heart on the spot. But a couple of months later, we began dating. We fell in love, and next thing you know I was planning our wedding. I was only twenty years old, but I meant what I said when I vowed to love and to cherish till death do us part.

When I was little, my parents divorced. That event ended my worry-free childhood. It was painful. And it continues to be painful, so I believe I know how young people feel when they experience the split of their families. That is why I have always worked so hard with Bob to ensure that Nick and all of our children grow up with two parents, committed to each other. "Till death do us part" is a pledge that means what it says to me.

Bob and I were *not* in any financial position to have a child. Still, both of us wanted a baby right away. My fractured family probably had something to do with it. But I only knew that I wanted a baby.

Pregnant—Growing Out but Determined Not to Stay Down

Doctors say that all babies in the womb are influenced by the sounds and the rhythms in their mother's environment. If that's true, then it's no wonder that Nick and all my other children enjoy rocking so much! But I'm getting ahead of myself a bit.

Bob and I lived in a tiny house owned by his mother, Barbara. It was way out in the country, near the small village of Stedman, New York. Our neighbors were all related to Bob's family one way or another. So there I was, isolated on a little country road, a newlywed still for all intents and purposes, a first-time mother-to-be, and alone most of the time. My husband was gone all week, driving his truck to far parts of the United States. If I was lucky, I saw him on Saturdays and Sundays. A lot of the time, he says, he had some version of the truckman blues; I simply had a strain of the blues directly connected to being left behind and lonely.

I turned to the one thing that always gives me comfort, music. Bruce Springsteen was one of my favorites. I was a big fan. At that time, Springsteen's music was not in the mainstream, not to everyone's taste. That included my husband. Bob didn't like listening to Bruce. Let me point out he did change his mind when the *Born in the USA* album was released. I liked to listen to Elvis Costello, Kiss, Foghat, Foreigner, and Lynyrd Skynyrd. I began to enjoy some of Bob's favorite artists, too. I listened to Linda Ronstadt, James Taylor, and Fleetwood Mac.

With Bob gone and no neighbors nearby, I could turn the music up as loud as I wanted. And boy, was it loud sometimes! I am inclined to think that my choosing music as my boredom-buster played a first big part in making Nick turn out to love it so. But, then, he was also exposed to music from the moment of birth. . . .

I needed more than listening to music to keep me occupied and amused. I've always been physically active. In high school, I ran track. I was the only girl on the team. I was an early feminist. I didn't outrun the other boys, but I was the coach's secret weapon. My male teammates ran faster just so they wouldn't get outrun by a girl!

What kind of physical activity could my growing tummy tolerate, an exercise that I could manage alone, without a lot of space? Ours wasn't a big house by any means. And winter was upon us, so I was cabin-bound, as Western New Yorkers in the snow-belt sometimes are during bad winters.

So I began to dance, alone, around the house. This combined my love for music with my determination to get physical and stay healthy while my baby was growing. It seemed a perfect solution, because there was no one to look into my windows and conclude that I had lost it! Actually, I found it—a way to beat my loneliness and pass the hours that seemed end-less.

I danced in the living room on the day I went into labor. I was due to deliver our baby around January 20. Back then they didn't give mothers-to-be sono-grams the way they do now, so I didn't know for sure if I was carrying a boy or a girl. I'll make a confession, though. If I'd had a girl first, I would have been slightly disappointed. I had my mind set on having a boy first, then a few years later giving birth to a little sister for him to play with. I'm delighted with how our family turned out.

In any event, I was getting impatient—to put it mildly!—by the time January 27 rolled around. I was downright sick and tired of walking around, that is, waddling around and lying down with this humongous belly. To say I felt like a Volkswagen Beetle had attached itself to my tummy wouldn't be too far off the mark. So on the night of the twenty-seventh I decided to give nature a little boost, my baby a little help in deciding when to come out.

Music was the midwife at Nick's debut into this world. That afternoon, I put on Bruce Springsteen's "The Promised Land," an optimistic working-class song in which he sings about life and how it's going to get better. I shared those sentiments. And I danced. I even did a few jumping jacks. Maybe I should contact Bruce sometime and thank him because, the next day at eight o'clock in the evening, to my everlasting joy, little Nickolas Gene Carter was delivered into this world. My baby boy came bounding into the world, weighing eight pounds and fourteen ounces, nearly nine pounds. His birthday, coincidentally, is the same as my mother's.

And Bob was on hand for the birth. I didn't want to have the baby while he was off on the highway, out of touch. And he didn't relish the idea of stopping at pay phones, calling in frantically, worrying that he'd miss the event. So we tried to time it so that he'd be home, and he was. What a management feat!

All of the prospective grandparents were on hand, too, at the hospital in Jamestown. Nick was the very first grandchild in the family.

We decided to name our child Nickolas for several reasons. Christmas had passed not too long before, of course, so old St. Nick was an inspiration. I chose to spell the Nickolas with a *k* and not the *h* that is traditional. (At the time we liked to watch a popular television show called *Eight Is Enough*. The youngest star in that rollicking brood was named Nicholas, and he caught our fancy.) To the Nickolas, we added Gene. This was for Bob, as it is his middle name.

Reinventing Ourselves

Being a mother, holding my tiny Nick in my arms, was everything I imagined motherhood would be. Nick was a delightful baby in every way, sweet and happy. But life was far from perfect for us. There's an old saying that goes something like *Necessity is the mother of invention*. For us, motherhood and father-hood made it necessary for us to reinvent ourselves.

After Nick was born it was even harder having Bob gone all week driving his truck. In the rural area in which we lived, though, good jobs were very hard to find. If you didn't drive a truck, work in the gas fields, or in one of the factories, there wasn't much oppor-tunity for a person without a lot of education. Service jobs were available, but only in the summertime, and they didn't pay a living wage. I had gone to college to become a dental assistant, but the closest jobs for me were in Jamestown, which was some distance away. And honestly, I really wanted to be home to raise Nick myself. I couldn't stand the thought of leaving him in day care.

The prospect of being separated from Nicky was disheartening enough, but then my husband's health began to be a problem. Bob had a history of stomach disorders. The stress of a new family to take care of while being on the road all the time was just too much. His condition worsened and required a doctor's care. Bob went on disability.

This began a very trying time for us. For a long period, which I will never forget, we barely had enough money to survive. To pay for our necessities we were forced to rely on food stamps and the WIC program for Nick's baby formula.

Bob and I were, are, and always have been extremely proud. We felt that for every problem that pops up, there must be a solution. You can't give up. You have to keep searching until you find your answers. Feeling that it is vital to stand on your own two feet, we decided that the ideal solution for us was to go into business for ourselves. Then we could be together. We could be there for Nick, to enjoy him as a baby and to watch him grow.

We admitted that our solution had a few not-so-insignificant snags. Number one, what type of business did we have the skills and the ability to launch? Number two, how were we going to finance a business?

We turned to Bob's parents. My mother-in-law worked in a factory. She and Bob's dad had worked hard all of their lives, saved, paid their bills on time, and always been financially responsible. They had a great credit rating. Bob was their only child. He decided to ask them to back us financially in a business venture, because just starting out, we had no chance of obtaining a loan. Their good credit enabled us to go into our restaurant/bar venture—Anthony's, a Main Street establishment in Westfield, New York. So off we went, plunging in with high hopes and light hearts.

Anthony's was really run-down. The building smelled overripe with mildewed paneling, due to filth from a thousand and one unwashed spots. It had bumpy linoleum flooring, covered with patches of mold. The yucky condition of the place had daunted prospective buyers, but not us. We were young and strong. Hard work didn't bother us. Bob and I turned ourselves into a Bob Vila and Martha Stewart duo and got down to the task of remodeling the club ourselves.

When we were finished, our club had its new look. It was time for a new name. We settled upon The Yankee Rebel because it paid homage to my in-laws' generosity and faith in us. Bob's mom was a Yankee and his father was a rebel from Tennessee. On our Yankee Rebel sign we even drew a caricature, Yosemite Sam, a good ole Southern boy carrying a shotgun. All we needed then were some customers—and lots of music.

In the beginning of the 1980s, we were smack-dab in the middle of the disco era. Now, you won't remember this, although if you watch *The 80's on MTV* you can see it for yourself, but disco music was quite a stretch from rock'n'roll. It was very controversial with as many fans loving it as disliking it. Donna Summer was the disco diva. Gloria Gaynor's "I Will Survive" became the classic disco anthem.

The Yankee Rebel was one of the few clubs in our semirural area where patrons could enjoy disco music. Bob and I had the nerve to play—and enjoy—it, even though the rock'n'rollers gave it the big thumbs down. Although we took a lot of flack, we didn't care. We didn't want a rock bar or a country-and-western saloon full of rednecks and rowdies. Disco music was evolving into what would soon be called dance music because of recordings like Michael Jackson's *Off the Wall* and *Thriller* albums, and Bob and I wanted a dance club that was upscale . . . and lots of fun.

We began booking the hot bands in our area. We became very influential on the local music scene. It was a small-town, close-knit musical culture. Only one publication reviewed all the latest musical acts. We advertised in it, keeping a close watch on who was up-and-coming. In time, the bands we booked became the musicians and singers that everyone in our neck of the woods was talking about.

We chose one local band, pretty well known, but not yet famous. You know them now as 10,000 Maniacs. Their lead singer, Natalie Merchant, has since established herself solo as a talented singer/songwriter, but back then the band got noticed, and their popularity skyrocketed, due to Natalie's intriguing sound on "Because the Night Belongs to Lovers." Natalie went to the local school in Westfield. Natalie learned poetry from one of my father's colleagues who taught English in the middle school. Small world, isn't it? I remember when Bob told me he was scheduling this band, I thought, when I saw the name, *What? You're going to book punk rockers for the club?* I admit his instincts were right on target.

We even brought acts down from Buffalo, some fifty miles up the road from us. Buffalo was a big city to us, but eighteen years ago it certainly wasn't the built-up metropolis that it is today. One of the bands we hired regularly, Ben Hatzel, was unique. The lead guitar player strummed his instrument not only with his fingers, but with his teeth and his toes! That was something to see!

Our club got the reputation of being *the* place to go. It wasn't long before other club owners started to copy our ways. Imitation is a compliment, I suppose. Life was busy. I found myself on the receiving end of a good education in the grass roots of the music business. This knowledge would certainly come in handy later on with Nick, but at the time I was more worried about what the club was doing to my baby.

A Different Drummer

Nick Carter always walked to the beat of a different drummer.

On a night in Germany in 1996, Nick was going to debut in a role that his fans were not accustomed to. Nick would be different, a drummer himself. Nick and the Backstreet Boys were performing at the Festival in Frankfurt concert that would become the video *Backstreet Boys Live in Concert.*

About three quarters of the way through the concert, the stage went dark. You couldn't see the fans but you could hear them screaming. Then from the middle of all this blackness a drum set rose from somewhere beneath the stage. Smoke billowed around it. Blue lights illuminated the drums. Then the spotlight picked up Nick, standing off to the side. He edged out toward the mysteriously appearing drums. Nick mimed. He looked around, rubbed his chin. *Should he or shouldn't he?*

Then he walked over to the drums, took a seat. Dressed in a Red Sox baseball shirt, he picked up the drumsticks. He struck the snares, thumped the bass with his right foot, shook his hair, curled his lips and began to play. *Wow,* I thought, *he sounds great!*

I wasn't surprised. At the start of the Backstreet Boys, we would spend a great deal of time at Lou Pearlman's home.

Nick first discovered his interest in playing the drums by stumbling on an old set in Lou Pearlman's garage.

Nick would always wander off to fiddle around with those drums. One day, Lou told Nick the drums were his.

Nick taught himself at first. If somebody can learn

to play the drums by ear, that's what Nick did. He picked it up naturally. When he and the boys finally had a live band backing up their act, he started taking lessons from the drummer. Nick's drumming really progressed rapidly. That night in Frankfurt, he was ready to perform professionally on drums. He played a great solo. Then he was joined by Kevin, and they previewed a new slow ballad called "Ten Thousand Promises."

That evening, Nick's drumming brought back the percussion lullabye that once upon a time jostled his crib. When he was an infant, we were living above The Yankee Rebel. We didn't have a kitchen in our apartment. I had to do all the cooking for us in the restaurant kitchen downstairs, which meant quite a bit of running up and down with Nicky in tow, riding my hip. As an infant he got used to being around people and music all the time.

On weekend nights, I would get a baby-sitter to stay with Nick while I ran downstairs to work. Simultaneously I mixed drinks and tapped beer as a bartender, flipped cheeseburgers and fried french fries as the cook, and served all of it to the customers as waitress. I filled in as a disc jockey, and even kept an eye out for trouble as a bouncer! I would slip away every hour or so to go upstairs to check on my baby boy.

It was during these frantic visits as Downstairs Jill of all trades/Upstairs mom that I would stand by Nick's crib and wonder how the sound and the vibration would affect him. Pulsating rhythm was the hand that rocked my Nicky's cradle. The bands played so loud that even the dishes in the cupboard rattled to the beat. The bass reverberated and hummed through the floor with such power that the walls vibrated and pulsated. I held on to the side of Nick's crib in those moments and could feel it literally trembling with the drumbeat.

Even though I was anxious when I looked down at my beautiful son, baby Nicky wasn't the least bit fazed. In fact he was always sound asleep, his little mouth curved upward in a smile. He seemed so peaceful. He never fussed. It was as if the boom and the thumping rocked him to sleep. The beat of the drums seemed to play harmoniously along with the rhythm of my baby's deep breathing. Undoubtedly, that is where Nick's urge to be a drummer was born.

During this past summer's tour, Nick took the drumsticks from the drummer to pound out "Quit Playing Games with My Heart." The beat goes on. . . .

Hey, Mr. DJ, Keep Playing This Song

Nick took his first steps in that family business, and another type of first step, too. He became an adventurous explorer.

When Nick started walking, life became a whole new ball game, as all mothers of toddlers quickly learn. At about the age of two, I started to bring Nick downstairs around our patrons more often. Two-year-olds need constant watching. By then, all our regulars knew little Nicky. He reveled in the extra attention he received from them.

On one evening in particular, Bob was spinning records in our DJ sound booth. I brought Nick downstairs. Fresh out of his bath and dressed, Nick was raring to go. Everyone danced away under the mirrorball, a huge silvery disco ball just like the one in the movie *Saturday Night Fever,* making the dance floor a magical setting. Strobe lights flashed, capturing my pint-sized Nick's image, as well as his fascination. The music boomed. Bob led Nick inside the booth. He took off his headset and put it on Nick so he could hear the next scheduled song.

Suddenly Nick grabbed both sides of the headset with his little hands and began pressing hard on his ears. I started to panic, thinking he was trying to free himself from the private concert playing into his head. I was afraid it might have been too loud. As I moved to take the headphones off, Bob stopped me.

He said, "No, wait a minute. I think he's enjoying it!"

This was one of those "Father knows best" moments. Nick flashed a smile that got bigger and bigger. He apparently loved the music funneling into his ears! I ran and got our camera, recognizing this as one of those Kodak moments.

Nick really grooved—and drooled, too, as toddlers do—to that music. You could just tell he loved this experience. He must have kept those headphones on for a good forty minutes before Bob was able to get them back for himself. I think most babies would have tired of this within seconds and taken off the headphones, but not my Nicky.

Whenever I'm at one of Nick's recording sessions, I flash back to that night! I see him again as a toddler with those headphones on. When I hear him sing "Hey, Mr. DJ, Play that Song for Me," I always recall my baby DJ the night Daddy played that song for him.

Disco Toddler

Nick's first wobbling steps were eclipsed only by his first dance steps in our club. If you are impressed with my Backstreet Boy's moves now, let me tell you how I was impressed from the tender age of two. There were times when I put Nicky out on the dance floor, and he just danced away with me. It was adorable to see the tiny toddler boogying to the music. When it came to twirling and dipping, twisting and stepping to the beat, Nick was a natural—even in diapers!

Playing Hide-and-Seek with Pac Man

During our stint in the music club business Nick discovered another one of his notorious loves—video games. The fan magazines always carry stories about how Nick even travels with his PlayStation so he can keep up the strength and speed of his video trigger fingers. When it comes to video games, he's a fierce competitor. It started before he was even two years old. Let me tell you about the exact day.

It was another of those times when I was running downstairs to cook while Nick napped upstairs in his crib . . . or so I thought. Bob was tending bar when I dashed up to look in on Nick. The crib was empty. Nick was nowhere to be found.

Frantically, I searched our apartment. In tears, I madly ran down the stairs and out into the alley. Ten thousand possible maniacs—not Natalie and her crew, of course, but the real kind—were dancing through my terrified maternal imagination. What had they done with Nick? I charged into the shop next door and asked anyone and everyone if they had seen a little blond baby boy. No one had.

Desperate, I rushed back into the bar to alert Bob. Dashing into the video room, I spotted Nick. There had been no kidnapping. No child snatcher had my precious baby in his clutches. Nick was happy as could be, safe and sound. He sat on a stool, playing a video game. On either side of him stood two ladies that we knew well, just as joyously feeding him quarters for the next round. All three of them were totally oblivious to the fact that up until that moment, I had been on the verge of a nervous collapse.

In many ways these were wonderful years for Nick, and for us as a family. But running a bar held some surprises. Nick was born to rock, and happy to roll with the music and the music scene. He would end up leaving the DJ headsets and his tiny dancing shoes behind, at least for a while. . . .

There's No Place Like Home

Home is what Nick really loves. I treasure this poem that Nick wrote during elementary school.

HOME
by Nick Carter

Home a place where I was born
A place to be comfortable a
Place maybe far but in my
Heart always over the rainbow.

Home always over the downs
And by the sea
And under the clouds
And in the breeze.

To watch a family
Learn and grow

To come home from school
To tell what I know.

But the one thing
That's best about home
It's always close
When you really need it.

A Guided Tour of the Places Nick Has Called Home

No matter where Nick lived, since the day he was born, Bob and I always made sure it felt safe, secure, and loving. Looking back at Nick's poem now, I understand as if for the first time how important home is to Nick.

The place where Nick hangs his hat these days—or should I say his baseball cap?—is a home fit for a segment on *Lifestyles of the Rich and Famous*. On that series, Robin Leach took his television audience right up to the front door and inside the ritzy mansions of the biggest stars from Hollywood to Palm Beach. Our Florida place isn't quite a Beverly Hills compound, but if MTV ever decided to do a rock'n'roll version, *"Lifestyles of the Rock'N'Famous,"* it would be a front-running candidate for the show. Fan magazines show pictures of our house. In one photo spread it was described as "fashionable digs," which clearly it is.

Our current home is the high point of our real estate history. Once, not terribly long ago, the only roof above Nick's head at times was the bright blue sky, and the main lighting fixture was the sun.

A Florida Dream House

At the end of a tour or a recording session Nick now comes home to the house of our dreams. It's one of the rewards of years of hard work and a proof that keeping your goals in sight can pay off.

Nick and I loved the house from the moment the realtor showed it to us. It had been abandoned for four years. The front yard was overgrown. It didn't have any lighting fixtures, but still it had the feel of a country home with its wood-beamed ceilings, stone fireplace, and sunken living room.

Now Nick and his brother and sisters live in a small town outside of Tampa. Our house is at the end of a suburban street, a dead end. A canal wraps around our property. To come into our home you drive through a tall black wrought-iron gate with an intercom.

Nick's rising popularity turned our home into a tourist attraction. One day recently when Nick was to arrive from a tour, we had about a hundred people outside with banners welcoming him back. Aside from that one particular home-coming event, we usually get about fifty fans a day for whom we always have autograph cards available. Nick wants them handed out as a token of his appreciation that a fan would take all the time and trouble to see his home.

When Nick is home he sometimes ambles out and personally says hi. When he or any of my other children go down to the mailbox, there's often somebody with a video camera ready to tape.

Let me open the gate for you and take you up our circular brick driveway. Our home is a modern beige and brown version of a country-style design. Florida palms and tropical plants sway in the balmy breeze to greet you. In back there's a crooked palm tree that boaters can see as they glide along the canal.

Our living room is decorated like many of yours, with soft wall-to-wall carpeting and comfy couches. And yet it is unmistakably the home of a pop star. A collection of platinum records from sales in countries all around the world fills the walls. These shimmering showcases of framed discs start at ground level and continue right up to our high ceiling. Everywhere one looks—on our

 As one of the Backstreet Boys, Nick has earned coveted MTV awards and also elegant sculptured trophies from foreign music organizations. One of those trophies was presented to me for giving the world not one, but two pop stars!

coffee tables and bookcases—there are awards, accolades, and mementos from many sources.

In between the gifts from people in the music business are presents from Nick's fans. They have places of honor in our living room. There are some spectacular photographs of Nick singing and wonderful, whimsical caricatures all sent to us by talented young fans. There isn't room to feature each and every gift, but we try to display as many as possible because they mean so much to Nick and to all of us in the Carter family.

Even celebrities like Nick stand in awe of some famous peers. Cindy Crawford autographed her photograph for Nick, signing "Happy Birthday." It's on a coffee table.

Nick and Aaron share a loft bedroom that Bob had a hand in building. Nick's the messier of the two, but now that Aaron is soon to be a teen, he's catching up fast. I think it's the age. When kids become teenagers, they seem to spend a little less time on neatening up their rooms. Nick's large bed is covered with a bedspread that's green—his favorite color.

Onstage singing and dancing, Nick gets bombarded with items, some of which find their way into his bedroom. **Fans hurl teddy bears and a regular menagerie of stuffed cats, dogs, sharks, and Beanie Babies at Nick and the other Backstreet Boys. Nick plays catch, and coos with the flying furry friends. A sampling of his favorites, saved from these concerts, lines the floor just underneath a series of windows that run along one wall of his bedroom.** He sees them every time he looks out his window at the serene view across the canal.

Nick has a huge walk-in closet with lots of hanging space and shelving. Hockey jerseys line up next to jeans and shorts. The top shelf boasts a collection of hats. There are baseball hats from teams coast to coast, and funny hats, too varied even to describe. Many of them have come from fans. Nick loves wearing them. There's a mess of computer game paraphernalia, PlayStation consoles and wiring, and some valuable collectibles. Over the years Nick played with baseball cards, as many young adolescents do, and there's quite a boxful. Basketball is Nick's favorite sport, and he has a prized basketball autographed by the athletes he admires.

Yes, even though Nick is a teen idol, he is also a real teenager. His bedroom holds all the evidence of an adolescent who still has a tiny toehold in childhood. When he comes home, he takes out everything, making a colossal chaos with stuff strewn all over the floor. You'd think a tornado set down.

> Jokingly, Nick teases, "I'm not home much. So when I am, I feel obligated to mess up my room."

Even with that charm and smile Nick can't weasel out of trouble all the time. Several months ago after Nick pulled one of his usual homecoming hurricane maneuvers, Bob told him he needed to clean up his room because people were coming to visit. Nick didn't clean his room, so he got grounded! Did the superstar throw a super-protest? No. Actually, I think he was secretly pleased that we still pay attention to what he does and that he's a regular member of the family. Nick is like any teenager, and I believe that teenagers tend to think you don't care if you never discipline them when it's called for.

Part of the decor of our home stems from Nick's fame; part of it honors the achievements of others. Some fans may be wallpapering their rooms with posters of Nick; Nick plasters his room with posters of Michael Jordan.

When Nick is home, we can often find him out back—when he's not messing up his room—in an outdoor "study" that his dad built along the dock. It looks like *This Old House* meeting up with a hut from *Gilligan's Island*. It's a wooden enclosed room, with lattice walls, where the breeze blows in off the water. Our family loves sitting out there; it's where one of our family pets lives. A huge cage houses Baby Face, the iguana that Aaron loves to talk about. Our home has ample dock space for our boat. All of us, especially Nick, love to go out on the bay. We even have manatees swimming in our canal from time to time. We've posted a sign that warns PLEASE WATCH FOR MANATEES because they're endangered creatures here in Florida.

Our backyard also has a small but lovely tiled in-ground swimming pool. I've planted roses and lime trees all around the backyard. Nick and I don't have much time to smell the roses these days, but I love knowing that the fragrance of roses and pungent limes is blowing in the winds right outside. Also blowing in that wind is the sound of Nick's sisters and Aaron jumping on our family trampoline. We brought the trampoline with us to this house; it has quite a history. Nick's neighborhood notoriety began with his trampoline shows.

A fan asked me recently during an on-line chat,

"Does Nick feel like he is missing out on the everyday things that he could be doing at home?" My answer was yes. Sure he does. Nick enjoys traveling, but loves to be home.

Leaving the Yankee Rebel Behind

Nick's present address is as far away as you can possibly imagine from the address of his early days. Remember, our family didn't start out in a little house surrounded by a white picket fence. As you know, Nick learned to roll over to the beat of a real drummer when we lived on top of our club, The Yankee Rebel.

I learned by hard experience that the business of running a dance club doesn't promote peaceful and harmonious family life. The hours are long and arduous. I took little Nicky off the dance floor and up to bed early on many an evening, but the band played on. Many nights the musicians lingered after the band finished their final set and the customers strolled out. The musicians were revved up and full of the energy of putting on their show, even though it was a small-town one. Rather than feeling ready to get into their cars and head home, they needed to unwind.

I didn't understand the unwinding process then because Nick, my future showbiz headliner, was still in diapers. Our job was to get the musicians on their way. If that wasn't challenging enough, add the bevy of amorous young women, intoxicated by the music, the musicians, and the refreshments, who hung around. Sometimes we didn't get to bed until after 6:00 A.M.

I have to admit that Bob encouraged me to get to bed earlier than he often did. Could I get to sleep? An entirely different question. I would edge up the stairs and check on Nick. The look on his angelic face and his rhythmic breathing would banish my worries about him. But as I got into bed I would hear the commotion down below.

The worry meter started up again. After all, Bob remained downstairs alone, the sole proprietor. A room full of high-spirited people could lead to trouble and sometimes did. Bob would tell me all the details the next day. What he didn't know is that I already knew the details because I had stayed awake listening. I didn't drift off to sleep until I felt certain that a brawl had been quelled and that calm prevailed.

Our business made us want to sleep until noon. One small problem arose with regard to that pajamas and pillow fantasy: a bubbling bundle of blond energy who yelled "Mom" from his crib. After all, by early morning Nicky had had plenty of *zzzz*'s, sleeping soundly with rock'n'roll as his lullabies.

Gypsies, Tramps, and Thieves

I wanted a different life, a better life for Nick. Bob's mom came to help us, but adding another strong-willed woman to our routine wasn't the answer either. After some serious soul-searching, when Nick was barely two, Bob and I whisked him off on an adventure. Our destination for a fresh start—sunny Florida.

We packed all of our belongings and our dog—a black Doberman named Sabbath—into a blue Dodge van and a camper. Nick, Bob, and I were the three amigos. We may have been short on funds but we had no shortage of the optimism of youth. We linked up with another adventurous couple and planned to get jobs, pool our money for rent, and live happily ever after basking in the Florida sun.

We drove over the Florida line with Nick sleeping soundly in the back. We made it to Tampa, then Orlando, and set up housekeeping in a little campground, living like gypsies, you could say.

I had a playpen that I set up outdoors for Nick to play in during the day. The ceiling of his playroom was the sky. At night I tucked him into a makeshift bed in the back of the van, where he looked up at the stars through the van windows. Sabbath curled next to Nick, guarding him in a snoozing duet until dawn.

Bob and I took a series of temporary jobs, and we lived a vagabond life. I motorcycled to a hostess job at a restaurant, carrying my uniform and doing a quick change before my shift. I washed Nick's little undershirts and our laundry in the sink of a local gas station. On a clothesline that we strung on our site, our wardrobe billowed and baked in the sun. We dined hibachi-style as the sun went down.

Nick thrived in the fresh air. We were all young and healthy. The outdoor life was fine for us. Our neighbors felt otherwise. Understandably, they did not appreciate these gypsies invading their territory, and they told us so in no uncertain terms. We ignored their snobbishness, choosing to focus on our happiness in sunny Florida. We believed we deserved our rightful share of the American Dream and let their ill will slide off our backs.

With paychecks from my work at the restaurant and Bob's new trucking job with Florida Rock and Gravel, we rented a house in Apopka. We could afford the rent, but at first we had no money left to buy furniture or pay for electricity. So in the beginning of our Apopka sojourn, I fed Nick McDonald's Happy Meals by candlelight. He can't recall how he happily chomped on cheeseburgers and french fries in the glow of a candle, but I sure can, and the memory makes me smile.

Putting Nick to sleep without a bed, into a sleeping bag on the floor, bothered us . . . and then one night Bob and I spied a neighbor hauling a mattress out to the curb. We waited until it got dark. Like some version of Bonnie and Clyde, Bob and I drove up, jumped out, tossed the mattress onto the roof of the van, and sped away like thieves in the night with our prized booty for little Nicky. The next night we proudly drew fresh-smelling sheets under Nicky's chin as he snuggled into his "new" bed.

The First Girls Who Hurt My Nick

Better days lay ahead, we felt certain.
I applied for a new job at a local convenience store

just down the street from our new home. I wanted to be closer to Nick. I felt certain I'd get that position. Dutifully, I took the lie detector test required when applying at that store. When asked if I was pregnant, I told the truth and admitted that possibly I was. Immediately I got word that I could not have the job. This was long before pregnant women had recognized rights. Worse, I had quit my other job, because I was so certain I'd be hired. Things were not going well.

I had a teenage baby-sitter to care for Nick while I worked. Not having enough money to open a bank account, we stashed our cash in a baby food jar. I wrapped this nest egg, our rent savings, in remnants of fabric and hid it among my sewing supplies in our spare bedroom. That room contained some twenty boxes filled with our household belongings, which patiently waited for bureau drawers. I came home on my last day of work and looked for the rent money.

It was gone. Stolen! The baby-sitter denied knowing anything about the missing money, as did her six-year-old sister, who often accompanied her. I knew they were lying. The convenience store owner who took two twenty-dollar bills in return for candy and sodas from them over the next few days backed up my suspicions.

I may have been right, but it made no difference. Bob and I were broke. I was jobless, Nick was without a sitter, and I was pregnant. The three amigos, now with heavy hearts, had to saddle up and head back home to New York.

The Pleasant View Retirement Home

At first our homecoming proved dismal. Bob and I went back into the bar business with his mom. We divided up the bar and opened our own nightclub, Centerfold Lounge. Then I got some excellent advice. Next stop, a lovely Victorian home in Westfield, New York.

Being back in the bar business was my worst nightmare. I confided my dismay to one of our regular customers whom I befriended. While bartending in the evenings, many times I talked to my new confidante, Jan. I told her how I wanted more. I envied Jan because she owned her own business and didn't appear to be struggling as we were. She ran a retirement home, called The Stepping Stone. That name proved to be prophetic for Nick, Bob, and me.

Knowing how unhappy I was in the nightclub business, Jan inspired me, and encouraged me to start up a retirement enterprise of my own. She advised me every step of the way, and even helped to line up my first resident. I knew it wouldn't be easy, but I was determined to succeed. I had to because I wanted to give Nick and the baby on the way a better life. Bob and I took our responsibility to our family seriously.

With a small loan, which my father co-signed, and sheer willpower, I scoured the area and found a large, lovely, white Victorian home. It had eight large bedrooms and the most romantic wraparound porch you could imagine. The kitchen was huge and the dining room seemed endless. The house had fireplaces everywhere. Nick had his own room as did his new baby sister, Bobbie Jean Carter, born January 12, 1982.

The Carters reinvented themselves. We were in the home health-care field. Our licensed family home for the elderly was called The Pleasant View Retirement Home. Soon four elderly boarders joined us, forming a kind of extended family for us. We could have dinner together every night in our dining room as a family, including our newest oldest members, and holiday celebrations in the living room, complete with fires in the hearth.

Florida Was Lovelier the Second Time Around

Bob and I were raising Nick and BJ, as we call Bobbie Jean, in New York, but not in a happy New York state of mind. We wanted to be back in Florida, combing its beaches for seashells, wiggling our toes in the warm sand. How did we wind up in Florida again?

One of our residents, Helen, with whom we were especially close, grew weaker. She needed assistance to get in and out of bed. Our license didn't allow us to care for those kinds of clients. Helen had to leave us for a nursing home. Nick missed her terribly; he felt as if he'd lost a grandmother.

Helen loved Florida as much as we did. She spent much of her youth vacationing there. I was reminded of that fact each day when I moved the plastic orange tree that stood on her nightstand to dust around it. She'd often showed me her prized postcard collection of beautiful Florida scenes. Nick loved looking over these with her as well.

Because of Helen's exile and our mutual longings for Florida, I decided that the ideal solution for everyone would be for us to buy a retirement home in Florida. Why not?

We chose Tampa, located on the Gulf of Mexico. I telephoned some local realtors. Indeed, a listing existed that seemed just right. Bob hopped an airplane to Tampa to investigate. And very soon Nick's next address was The Garden Villa, a Home for the Elderly.

When I first saw this house, its plainness stunned me a bit. Still, it was set back nicely on a quiet street with a lush canopy of trees shading it. A porch attached to the outside did have lots of potential. We got it at a good price because it needed tons of work. Immediately we set out to change this house, which didn't have the tiniest shred of atmosphere or warmth, into a real home. We had exactly what this place needed, though: the addition of a family, the energy of my blond bomber and bombshell, and a handyman husband, too.

When the repairs and painting were finished, I hung up lots of pictures and put fresh flowers in several of the rooms. With a few more decorations, we had transformed the house into a real home with a distinct family feeling.

What they say about the power of the woman's touch is all true. Nick and BJ spent the next few years playing happily in his private little rainforest–like setting.

After a few years, with the addition of our newest daughter, Leslie, we outgrew The Garden Villa. We hired a couple to live in the retirement home while we moved Nick and our daughters across the street to a lovely ranch house. We took Nick and his sisters to work with us each day, until they were old enough to attend school.

The white stucco home resembled a typical Florida house. It had a large cropped front lawn, trimmed with tropical shrubbery. A large cement driveway became a great place for Nick and his sisters to ride their bikes or play.

Number 216 remained the home where Nick grew into a child star. That was the house where, when I tucked Nick in at night, he first whispered his starstruck fantasies to me just before lights out.

When we lived in that home, heading across the street to the retirement business and our extended family there, Nick and I dreamed only of success, and not of the grander homes that might go along with it.

When Nick, at fifteen, signed his recording deal, we made plans to move.

Today Nick and I along with the rest of our family live happily in a spectacular residence, one that dreams did indeed build. Nick doesn't get to spend as much time as he would like to at this most recent address. He's off with his Backstreet Boys traveling the world.

The Carter real estate history has featured places by the sea and, yes, even spots under nothing but the clouds. Breezes blew in and out of a number of bedroom windows for my growing superstar. The poet in my son has aged, but his feelings about home are ageless.

No matter where Nick hangs his baseball cap, his heart will always yearn for home. A world traveler, yes, and a homebody, too.

4

Nick's Family Tree . . . ☆ and How the Apple ☆ Didn't Fall Far

Rock stars are America's royalty. Nick and AJ, Madonna and Mariah, the celebrities who sell millions of CDs are our modern-day kings and queens. It is only fitting that the princes and princesses, sitting on thrones of celebrity, dress in the finest threads. When Nick is home in Tampa, it's usually bare feet and a bathing suit for him, but it's definitely designer duds in public. Donatella Versace dressed him for his recent appearance at the MTV Music Video Awards, the Oscar night for the young, hip, and in.

Being treated like royalty takes some getting used to for Nick. Versace clothing, top-notch hotel suites, and stretch limousines are a long way from his humble beginnings. Then along comes Nick's grandfather, my father, Douglas Spaulding, who tells us Nick has anything but humble beginnings.

Nick's granddad traced our family roots. Nick Carter's pedigree has been tracked back two thousand years. Nick is part Scotch, English, Irish, Welsh, French, Dutch, and German. That's why Nick says he is so many things when asked about his ethnic background.

Grandfather Spaulding became interested—"obsessed" might be a better description—in genealogy after he retired. What he has turned up is fascinating and goes a long way toward explaining the talents and ambitions that make Nick run.

Nick's lineage is anything but ordinary. It is downright regal, illustrious, and entertaining in more ways than one. Where does Nick get his good looks? Is musical talent demonstrated by his ancestors? What about showbiz aspirations? Was Nick the first in his family to set his sights on curtain calls and applause, or the latest in a long line of showbiz predecessors?

A Rock Star and a Riddle

Where does Nick get his many talents in art, in dance, in acting, and even in striking those captivating poses? The answer comes from climbing up Nick Carter's family tree. There we'll encounter grandmothers and grandfathers, aunts and uncles, and ancestors even further back, with creative flair, unusual stories, and yes, even historical significance. Well, maybe not *all* had such significance, but even their stories have a bit of entertainment value.

Here's a riddle. What do you get if you cross a beauty pageant winner, a pipe organ virtuoso, a Shakespeare fanatic, a portrait artist, a classical pianist, and a couple of disco entrepreneurs and music lovers? Nick Carter!

Let's start with beauty. Nick's handsome face is no fluke. Nick's great-grandmother, Teresa Spaulding, nabbed first prize in a beauty pageant back in 1931. It may not have been the Miss America contest on the boardwalk in Atlantic City, but Teresa's wavy hair, curvy proportions, and sparkling smile rivaled the best of the beauties in her day. On that afternoon at the competition at the old Rex Theater in Cory, Pennsylvania, Teresa sauntered past a line of judges in her swimsuit, wowed them all, and walked off with the crown. Miss Cory 1931, modestly quoted years afterwards about her accomplishment, "I was born under a lucky star." Apparently she was shy when people commented on and praised her physical attributes.

Nick inherited more than her lucky star. He gets just as embarrassed, and has been known to blush, when someone tells him how downright gorgeous he is. Onstage Nick

He may sing the musical question and act like "Mr. Am I Sexual?"—with throngs of girls assuring him he is—but in real life you won't catch Nick preening in front of the mirror or even giving much thought to those movie star looks.

preens in the "You're So Vain" tradition of Mick Jagger. Lots of people, like Regis Philbin, have teased him about resembling Leonardo DiCaprio. Nick shrugs off such comparisons.

There's further evidence that beauty runs in the Carter genes. Nick's sister, BJ, repeated Great-Grandma Teresa's feat, walking off the runway with the Miss Tampa tiara. But in the Carter family, physical beauty doesn't count for much. A beautiful girl must also have a beautiful soul, and a tender, compassionate heart. It's what's on the inside that counts. Sounds familiar, I know. **When you hear Nick talk about what he admires in a girl, his remarks always imply that beauty is only skin deep. Of course Nick finds good-looking girls attractive. How else would you expect a red-blooded teenager to react?** And yet, good looks aren't enough if goodness is missing. Miss Cory 1931 celebrated her eightieth birthday some years back, and when her large extended family gathered around to celebrate, they talked of the kind of beauty that doesn't fade. Beauty is in Nick's genes, but so is keeping it in perspective.

Nick's grandmother, my mother, Helen Jean Neal, taught kindergarten. Everyone spoke about her bright intellect, but it was something else that people admired. Her most popular gift was music. She played wonderful classical piano, including Bach, Beethoven, Brahms, all the great piano composers. Helen was a child prodigy on her instrument. My childhood was filled with sounds of her classical music, which I enjoyed enormously. But I also was

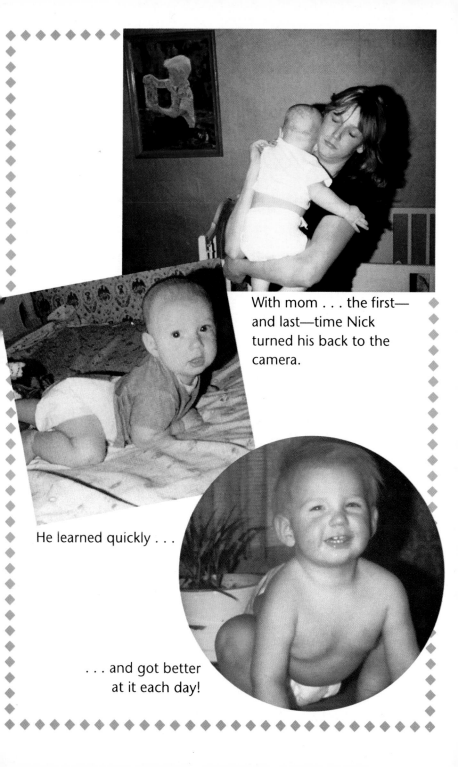

With mom . . . the first—and last—time Nick turned his back to the camera.

He learned quickly . . .

. . . and got better at it each day!

Disco toddler.

A born DJ.

Standing behind Nick . . . always.

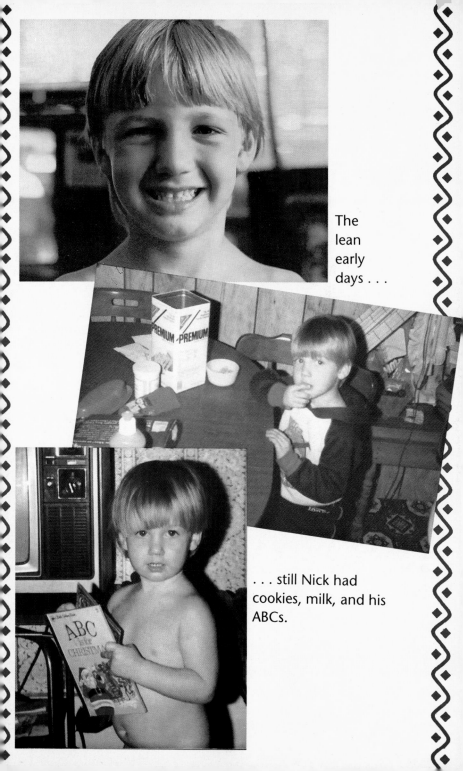

The lean early days . . .

. . . still Nick had cookies, milk, and his ABCs.

by Nick, age 6

When the family finally settled in the Sunshine State, there was lots of time and opportunity for
**FUN
IN FLORIDA**

Helen teaches Count Dracula his letters, not his "numbers."

Even the school photographer couldn't dim this
eight-year-old's smile.

Nick and his beloved Sabbath . . .

. . . and sorting out toys for Aaron.

Eleven years old—and already looking like a polished star.

Grandfather Douglas posing with Bob and me.

There's no better Christmas present than a happy family.

When I was a teenager I painted this picture of a blond boy with butterflies in a jar . . . a premonition?

The big day for Bob and me.

Nick

Cool...

. . . hot!

The once and future star.

exposed to and enthusiastic about pop, jazz, and rhythm and blues. Helen certainly had enough talent, but never chose to go into music professionally. Of all her intellectual and creative gifts, art was her favorite. She majored in art in college. Whenever I see Nick doodling with a pen, or working seriously with colors to create his cartoon characters and superheroes, I think of my mother drawing or painting, and of myself doing the same. I'm in the middle of creating a children's book for which I'm doing both the text and illustrations.

Nick's great-grandfather, Robert Neal, mastered the organ. Self-taught, Robert played the huge pipe organ in the Pittsburgh Presbyterian Church and directed the choir there for many years. He had considerable strength—and he needed it, for the pipe organ is played as much with the feet as with the hands. The foot pedals have to be pressed hard and steadily for the sound to swell properly. That takes strength and stamina. It's remarkable how he could develop his muscles and his powers of endurance. Because of an illness during his youth that severely and permanently damaged the veins in his legs, he had to treat and bandage his legs every day of his life. Still, he tackled the foot pedals with gusto. He had to overcome many other obstacles, too.

At a very young age, Robert lost his father in a traumatic way. His father worked at a store, and part of the responsibility of his job was to take each day's receipts to the bank for deposit. But on one fateful day, a robber lay in wait, shot and killed the young father, and made a successful getaway. The murdering thief was never brought to justice.

Great-grandfather Robert was a near genius, extremely well-read, and a great admirer of the music of Johann Sebastian Bach. He recognized Nick's vocal gifts early on. Nick sat next to the piano and Great-Grandpa played. "Amazing Grace" was the first song Nick learned from him. He died at eighty-nine but if he were alive today, I doubt he'd be at all amazed by Nick's success.

Nick, and now Aaron, weren't the first on the family tree to join or start bands as young adolescents. A great-grandfather named Harry had a band when he was a teenager. He even composed, but love changed the tune. One of his turn-of-the-century admirers was a beautiful young woman with whom he fell in love. They married and soon she was pointing out that music, although fun and fulfilling, did not put bread on the table. So even though Harry could play nearly every musical instrument, he agreed to find a more profitable profession. True to his word, he never picked up one fiddle or flute again. Luckily, Nick's fate is far different. He can make money doing what he loves. But we have to hope he doesn't fall in love with a girl who doesn't support his career. We wouldn't want to see him retire his microphone or drums!

One of Nick's recent ancestors was among the best violinists of the last generation, Albert Spaulding. Thomas Edison recorded one of Albert's string performances. Apparently a light bulb went off in Edison's head one day when he heard Albert's fiddling. He thought Albert's bow played the purest sound and would be useful in his experiments with sound recording. Apparently, it was. Albert won music competitions at such a young age that controversy erupted. Was he too young to qualify for the prizes? Like Mozart, he was a child virtuoso. With ancestors like this, it's no wonder that Nick's musical genes revealed themselves almost from day one!

Some families have enough kids to make a basketball team. One of Nick's ancestors, Daniel, had ten sons who all played violin, so he had the makings of a full string section.

Tin Pan Alley is famous for its songwriters. Nick had an ancestor who aspired to get there. A great-aunt named Anna considered herself a poet and a songwriter. Once upon a time, Anna actually got the opportunity to meet Bing Crosby. Anna used this fortunate audience to pitch him one of her songs. Its title was "The White Hills of New Hampshire." Never heard of it? The fact that we still hear Bing's "White Christmas" and that we don't ever hear him singing "The White Hills of New Hampshire" tells you that her pitch didn't succeed as she had hoped. (You know what they say, though. It wasn't the quality of the song; Anna just didn't find the right singer to appreciate it.)

Nick got a movie script when he was backstage in New York City recently. It wasn't the first script that crossed his desk or that someone plunked into his hand. Nick has had roles in several movies. You have to be sharp to catch his performance in *Edward Scissorhands*. He slips and slides on a front lawn so quickly you have to know what to look for or you might miss him! Nick had a more serious role in an HBO movie called *The Judgment*. Acting is in the family bloodline, too.

Grandfather Douglas always loved dramas and throughout his life he's acted in community theater. He is a huge fan of Shakespeare. In fact, while auditioning for Gilbert and Sullivan's *The Mikado,* Douglas met his future wife, my mother, Helen, who also was trying out for a part in that operetta. They married, becoming each other's leading lady and man. Douglas fancies himself a playwright. He's been working hard, if only part-time, for quite a while on a script about Shakespeare's final days.

Singers belting out hymns in the choir loft on Sunday mornings . . . singers gathering around pianos in the afternoon . . . violinists playing dueling classical banjos . . . songwriters picking out melodies . . . playwrights and actors pounding the pavement. As you scale the limbs of Nick's family tree, you can see them all. Equally important, Nick, his brother, and sisters have been raised in a creative climate. Sitting around the piano, listening to impromptu concertos, or joining in a songfest is the sound of Carter family holidays. Our walls are makeshift art galleries, displaying all our current sketches, drawings, even fingerpainting.

Plymouth Rocks

When Nick first traveled to Europe, he's said that he felt as if he were setting out to conquer the world of music. Perhaps he was merely reversing the trip taken so long before by ancestors from the Old World. Nick's lineage has been meticulously traced to those original, golden settlers who came to America on the *Mayflower*. Over forty-five connections of Carter, Spaulding, Phillips, and Crippen *Mayflower* ancestors have been proven. Apparently, Nick rocks all the way back to Plymouth Rock.

Genealogy is a complex tracking of crisscrossing family lines. In the elaborate antique family tapestry that this genealogy uncovered were well-known legends from virtually every field—the arts, law, politics, business. Eli Whitney, the cotton gin inventor; Henry Wadsworth Longfellow, legendary American poet; J. P. Morgan, early financier and millionaire; Oliver Wendell Holmes, renowned Supreme Court Judge; millionairess Marjorie Post and her daughter, actress Dina Merrill; George Bush, forty-first president of the United States—all intersect with the present-day Spaulding Carters. These are a few of the luminaries who would gather at a family reunion that rightfully includes an appearance by Nick Carter. Celebrity runs in his ancestral lines.

Nick was born in the same hospital where Lucille Ball came into this world. That celebrity tidbit pales in comparison to Nick's very real connections to very celebrated people of the past.

Will Nick—Like Elvis—Join the Army?

From time to time Nick expresses an interest in joining the military. It's hard for me to imagine him in uniform, but not hard to imagine that he'd be one of the most physically fit enlisted men ever to start basic training, thanks to the dance workouts ordered by choreographer Fatima. Would Nick trade in his Skechers for army boots? How about a razor-toting sergeant shaving off Nick's blond hair? Nick without that beautiful, thick, gleaming hair? Stranger things have happened to rock idols, I suppose. And there was Elvis, who exchanged his guitar for a rifle, was shipped over to Germany, and did a tour of military duty that was a far cry from a concert tour.

Those military fantasies probably swirl around in Nick's head for lots of reasons—not the least of which is that there were so many military men on the family tree. One ancestor, Conrad Stuntz, a Prussian soldier trained in the art of war, came to American shores as a mercenary to fight in the Revolutionary War. He started helping the British. What happened next is disputed. Tales about burning ships and lost battles cloud the issues. But there's no doubt that Conrad switched sides and wound up helping General George Washington train his troops.

In the legendary Battle of Bunker Hill, the Spauldings were well represented, with disastrous consequences. Nine out of the ten who fought died, and the lone survivor escaped the others' fate quite by accident, it seems. He had been standing on the battlefield right next to General Prescott, as the leader sat perched high on his horse. The order "Don't fire till you see the whites of their eyes" rang out as the enemy came up over the hill. Spaulding heard a cannon blast; impulsively and against orders he fired his gun. The general smacked him on the head with his sword. The jumpy sniper with the itchy trigger finger was knocked out cold. The battle raged all around him that day. He appeared dead, and so soldiers stepped over him. When he came around, he discovered sadly that of all the Spauldings who had fought that day, he alone had survived.

Nick's grandfather Douglas, the genealogy expert, is still working on our family history. He has other stories to tell that go back to Charlemagne and Alfred the Great. His tales of Nick's bloodlines range from the historical to the hysterical.

Here's one that has been recounted from the Carter-line elders that is more hilarious than illustrious. Family lore has it that one uncle fell in love with Lucille Ball. His *I Love Lucy* passion compelled him to follow Lucy wherever she went, even to the ends of the earth. Or so the romantic tale is told. Follow her he did, all the way to New York City. Did Lucy appreciate his ardor? Apparently she did not. The annals don't recount her side of the story, but I think that it's safe to say this Carter predecessor didn't have Nick's smile or his charisma. Nope, that fellow from long ago wound up sorely disappointed. Ms. Ball clearly didn't know there would be a song written called "I'll Never Break Your Heart."

Family stories like these float around on one side of Nick's family; his grandfather promises to get to work soon on the other side of the family, Nick's father's side. Heaven only knows how many more tall tales are out there waiting to be uncovered and retold.

Genealogy is quite a hobby. You never know what you will find out about yourself or your ancestors. Brushes with death or fame, matters of life and death, broken hearts and broken dreams, all kinds of plots and characters nestle in each person's family tree. If a number of people started researching their pasts, I bet at least one would discover some connection to the Carter clan, and even perhaps to the *Mayflower*.

Sometimes I ponder the origins of Nick's personality and talent. Who gets the credit for his movie star looks? Which ancestor is reflected in Nick's style and substance?

The past also holds a key to guessing what Nick might do next. After all, he is only eighteen. Will Nick join the military? Might he wind up singing and dancing in a Broadway production, maybe even writing some of its music or its dialogue? Nick is working on a comic book adventure, combining his talent for art with his interest in video games. Will there ever be an art gallery that exhibits the Nick Carter caricatures?

Nick has talents that he develops and uses now. As surely as his genetics promise, he has a multitude of other talents waiting to be developed and to move into the spotlight of his life.

5

How Watching MTV Changed the Carter Family

When Nick turned eighteen in January of 1998, he was not at home with us in Florida to celebrate his birthday. His sisters and brother, his dad, and I had to settle for cell phones and phone tag to get that Happy Birthday message to our busy traveling troubadour. I watched Nick on television, on MTV, where he was presented with a birthday cake complete with candles.

What a twist of fate! And suddenly I was remembering Nick's fourth birthday. MTV played a role at that celebration, too. In 1984, I baked the birthday cake, Nick's favorite. Atop the cake, five multicolored little candles glowed, four for each of Nick's years and the extra one for good luck. Bob turned off the lights, and with great fanfare I carried the cake out of the kitchen. Nick turned away from the television, which was tuned to—you guessed it—MTV, to blow out his candles. We turned down the sound on the television set while all of us Carters sang "Happy Birthday." As soon as our warbling ended, I started to cut the cake and Nick turned the sound back up. He was dying to hear and see the newest thing in entertainment: the MTV music video.

Nick and the Backstreet Boys have become a staple on MTV in the United States during this past year. The Backstreet Boys won European MTV's top honor, The People's Choice Award, two years in a row in 1996 and 1997. The climax for Nick of what could only be called a mutual-admiration-society-type of relationship with MTV occurred on September 10, at the 1998 Music Video Awards Show in Los Angeles.

Nick and his band mates starred in an opening spoof of themselves and their videos, done by Ben Stiller. During the program I watched as they performed their twice nominated music video "Everybody (Backstreet's Back)." Then Nick and the others walked off with the coveted "Planetman" trophy in the category of Best Group Video.

In the days leading up to the show, MTV handed a video camera to Nick and the group. Their assignment—direct themselves in a short film showing the MTV audience what goes on behind the scenes and leading up to this exciting night in rock. It aired as part of MTV's coverage.

Nick wanted TV viewers and fans to see life through the eyes of a Backstreet Boy. He turned the camera around as he walked into the pressroom with the award. What you see is a blinding, blinking explosion of flashbulbs all aimed at Nick and his band mates. It was a dramatic, live, flashing light show that could rock anybody. Rock stardom doesn't get bigger, more frantic, or more exciting than this!

A Nick-Mania News Flash for MTV

Well, I've got a scoop for the MTV VJs and the MTV music news reporters. It's a tale of how MTV changed Nick's life forever at a tender age. Those were the days when MTV was as much an infant as Nick. It's hard for teenagers to imagine a world before MTV, but, I assure them, there was one. (I'm afraid this makes me sound like my mother telling me about the early days of television.) Nick probably doesn't even remember this story, but I sure do.

Nick and I, his father, and sister BJ were living in the Pleasant View Retirement Home in western New York. That part of the country is smack in the heart of the snowbelt. It gets very, very cold in the winter. Arctic winds come down from Canada, across the Great Lakes, and sweep into this area of the Northeast, often dumping a foot of snow. It isn't unusual for snow to cover—actually, to bury—the ground from October or November until April and even into the first days of May. During record years one blizzard hits right after another. This is due to those lake-effect snows.

The winter of 1984 was full of snowstorms. Nick

and I lived through a winter that seemed endless. When I was a child, there were winters when the snow nearly reached the top of the telephone pole. I have a picture of my brother and me standing on top of such a snowfall with our hands touching the pole's top.

When you live through these kinds of winters, you know you are going to be trapped indoors for almost eight or even nine months of the year. When winter first begins, the snow is fun. In that winter of 1984, one cold night as the snow fell hard, I bundled little Nick and baby BJ in their snowsuits and sat them on a sled. I pulled them down the plowed main road. Town snowplows had piled the snow up a mile high on either side. New falling snow lightly swished around us and onto the ground. The night wasn't dark, but bright from the whiteness of the snow all around. The branches of all the trees glistened in the reflected light. The world was still except for the gentle patter of the falling snow. So the squeals of delight of my Nick and BJ sounded louder to me than normal. At moments like that our small town truly was a winter wonderland.

Unfortunately, those moments are short-lived. That winter wonderland bliss gives way to a bad case of cabin fever. Unless you're wild about snowmobiles or skiing, snowbound life is tough. Your days are measured in short excusions (once you dig your car out of the snow) to the grocery store, or to your job. You venture out with your body weighted down by layers of flannel and wool. Even with all that clothing, you shiver and rush to the warmth and security of the indoors. The sun goes down early. From the end of October, after you turn back the clocks, it's dark outside as early as 4:00 P.M. for what seems like months. That makes for a very long night.

The dark, the frigid world outside your door, the closed-in feeling—all these elements combine to make you feel trapped. The Carters wound up with a bad case of cabin fever just like many of our neighbors who hunkered down and tried to survive the long cold winter in the snowbelt in 1984.

Nick was an active child. He didn't have the kind of personality that lent itself to sitting still. He wanted to be out and about moving around his world. Keeping him inside during the winter was not fun for him or for me. What do you do with a bouncing boy of four who can't go outside at 5:00 in the afternoon because it is already dark—yet he doesn't go to bed for another four hours?

MTV to the rescue! We could never forget we lived in a nursing home. After dinner, as the evening progressed, the elderly patients needed their rest. Oftentimes they would go to bed early. Bob and I had to keep Nick and BJ amused and *quiet*.

Like countless other American families, we spent lots of time in front of the television set. I was young myself and

As we switched channels, we soon discovered that Nick loved watching MTV.

drawn to MTV, too. So was Bob. We didn't miss the nightclub business, but we still remained interested in the music business. We enjoyed following the artists who were the up-and-coming musicians and singers—but, even more, we got the biggest kick out of watching Nick dance to the music videos.

So after the day's work was done, Bob, Nick, BJ, and I would sit together and watch MTV almost every night. Unfortunately, the commercials that interrupted the videos tortured Bob and me. In our ice-bound dead of winter living room, we watched Florida vacation advertisements all the time. I still remember the wording of one commercial: "Florida! You need it bad!" Did we ever!

Considering our frigid, snowbound circumstances, these reminders of Florida struck us as downright cruel. Bob and I hadn't wanted to leave that sunshine state at all. Here we were, back in the deep freeze, "Eskimo Country" we often called it, watching MTV, and seeing tantalizing glimpses of palm trees, blue blue water, beaches—and sun! It was so depressing. All we did was eat and watch. We wished we could be back in the Florida warmth rather than being stuck here like human popsicles, ten feet deep in winter.

Life Can Be an Adventure

Here's where my philosophy of life helped thaw us all out once and for all. I believe that life is a series of changes. Sometimes things go the way you want them to; sometimes they don't. One always has the choice to make things better. It means that sometimes you have to take a chance. You have to believe there is light at the end of the tunnel, or in our case sunshine at the end of a blizzard. One windblown, snowbound day during the endless winter of 1984, I made a decision that would change our lives. I never wanted to build another snowman or shovel bricks for one more igloo.

I've already mentioned Helen, our first elderly patient in the nursing home, and how her health-care needs influenced us to relocate to Florida, but I want to add a few words about the importance to me of being adventurous. When I complained about the winter, and when Helen talked and we reminisced about Florida, and finally, when Helen left our family nursing home against all of our wishes, I decided to take action. I reached inside of me for that sense of adventure that my father instilled in me when I was young.

During my childhood days, my parents moved us back and forth across the country several times. My father was a schoolteacher. I was born in California, in a sleepy town called Brawley. My parents met at Pennsylvania State Teacher's College, near where my dad landed his first teaching job. Although he liked teaching, my father was young and he wanted to see other parts of the country and try different things. We lived in several places, Delano in the San Joaquin Valley, and Santa Barbara for a year. We moved to

Tempe, Arizona, where my dad went to graduate school at Arizona State University. Eventually, though, we wound up back in upstate New York.

You could say that my father, my upbringing, and my childhood experiences had put a little gypsy in my soul. So at this point in my life, with the cold, and the longing for a better life—and a warmer one, too—I tuned in to that pioneering spirit. I mustered the courage to head south. It was MTV that gave me the final push! All those Florida commercials did it.

As I look back now, I realize that MTV certainly played a bizarre role in Nick's life and mine. I wanted my MTV. Nick wanted his MTV. We all wanted our MTV, only we wanted it in a warmer living room setting.

Whenever I see Nick on MTV in the here and now, it often reminds me of our early years watching MTV. The people over at MTV have no idea about any of this Nick Carter history. And I doubt if Nick, when he walked down Broadway and up to the LIVE MTV Studio located at 1515 Broadway, gave this any thought. He was too young to make the connection between his stardom on MTV now and the influence that MTV and its music and commercials had on his childhood.

There really was a time, when to the beat of the music from MTV, the Carters decided to pick ourselves up, dust the snow off little Nicky's boots, and head south to start all over again.

6

Big Brother . . . and His Holding Company

This passage from the *I Ching* has always held special meaning for me.

> If the father is really a father,
> And the son is really a son,
> And the mother is really a mother,
> and the daughter is truly a daughter—
> The family is in order.
> And when the family is in order,
> The world is in order.

There's one home base where Nick spends tons of time—the tour bus. Nick got his first taste of living like a gypsy in our van on a Florida campsite at the age of two. These days he lives a vagabond life where the world passes him by at high speeds in a bus or an airplane. This past summer there was a new tour bus right behind Nick's Backstreet Boys sterling silver caravan. It was ten-year-old Aaron's; he opened the show. From cities like New Haven, Connecticut, and Baltimore, Maryland, our buses headed west crisscrossing America and then returned east through Canada. Hard to believe, but Nick is even more of a pop idol rage in Canada than in the U.S.

With his little brother on the road, too, Nick had the opportunity to hop onto Aaron's bus now and then to spend more time with him. One of the hardest sacrifices that Nick has made over the years is being separated from his younger sisters and brother. (You've heard him say that over and over again during interviews.) All of the Carter family members at one time or another over these last several years have bounced around in the tour bus with Nick. It was the only way to get to spend time with him.

And I do mean *bounce.* Part of chasing stardom for Nick meant living in the fast lane of a superhighway. Nick and his dad promise to write a history of those Backstreet Boys years. For now, Nick is not one to complain about life on the road. A tour bus is fascinating. It's a fairly steep climb up and into one of those huge streamline silver buses. The front space resembles a living room. On either side of the aisle there are couches. The interior decorator who designs the inside of these roving homes-away-from-home purposely adds domestic touches, such as kitchen curtains, warmly colored upholstery, and throw pillows. A VCR screen is attached to one corner of the ceiling so that the weary or hyper travelers can catch a movie.

A little breakfast nook is often off to one side, opposite a sink. A small refrigerator is built in underneath. Overhead are a few kitchen-style cabinets. On any given day, at least when I'm on board with Nick and Aaron and any of his sisters, the kitchen is stocked. A bowl of fresh fruit is affixed to the counter. There's plenty of bottled water and juice in the refrigerator. Having healthy snacks on hand is essential because more often than not meals are from fast-food restaurants.

The center portion of the tour bus is stacked on either side with bunks, as if one bunk bed was stacked on another bunk bed. It's tight. But when you are a rock'n'roll dancing machine and it's midnight, with seven hundred miles to the next town, a soft, warm sleeping bag in your own private little cubbyhole is pretty inviting. I've looked in on Nick, and on Aaron stacked underneath him. What I see are slightly older versions of the tiny boys I used to watch as they slept.

The back end of the bus is another living room section. More couches line either side. The television set is on the rear wall. Now on almost

Final Fantasy is Nick's favorite video game. I hear him and Aaron shouting and fiercely trying to battle the animated villains. It's a kill or be killed melee in the back of the bus.

any given day when Nick and Aaron are there, of course the TV is commandeered by the PlayStation.

The thousands of miles of a summer tour are broken up with stops in the heartland of upstate New York or off the road in Michigan. Nick leads Aaron out to a Wal-Mart or a Kmart, where they can check out the department store shelves for the newest video games, or stand on line and order a hot dog and a root beer. They have to move fast before anybody realizes that these two blond brothers aren't just local young adolescent shoppers, but superstars.

If living like traveling gypsies, stealing a summer afternoon out in the fresh air here and rumbling through a good night's sleep there sounds hard, that's because it is. Why would BJ, Leslie, or Angel want to sign on to this combination moving circus and cramped road show? Nick's brother and sisters volunteer for this tour duty, because they miss their big brother as much as they know he misses them. The extremely loving and close relationship among Nick, Aaron, BJ, Angel, and Leslie never wavers. There's footage about Janis Joplin, and Bette Middler's movie *The Rose,* which tells Janis's tale of rising to pop-star fame only to die so young, before she'd reached her peak. The Joplin band was called Big Brother and the Holding Company. Nick is and has always been the big brother, running his sisters' and brother's affairs like a company, with himself as the self-appointed director.

Bringing the Carter Family Album to Life

I have family photo albums overflowing with pictures of Nick and BJ, Nick and Leslie, Bob, Nick and the twins. So many capture candid moments of happy times our family has had. Several immortalize Nick managing his younger siblings or guiding their actions. Nick and I wanted to be able to show *all* of these photographs.

Unfortunately, we can't. Why? Neither Bob nor I, who took so many pictures of Nick and our other children over the years, are professional photographers. Although our family pictures feature Nick and BJ, Leslie, Aaron, and Angel, some are filled with shadows or distracting backgrounds. Many are dark. Still more are a little fuzzy or blurry. The process of printing them onto the pages of this book would make them even darker or murkier.

Just as I was thinking *What a shame!* I came up with a solution. I can't show a picture that says a thousand words, but I can write a thousand words to draw these pictures for you. I'm going to describe the action within nearly half a dozen pictures. As I do, you will see how Nick nurtured his siblings, directed them, sometimes just like a famous movie director, and led them into adventures and even shenanigans. The last "picture" Nick himself will tell you about.

Nick at Three and a Half Pushing His Baby Sister on a Swing

When Nick was just two and three, he behaved very affectionately toward BJ. From the start, the two of them were kissing and hand-holding coconspirators in family mischief, whether it was sticking their fingers in the chocolate icing of a birthday cake I baked and finger-painting chocolate mustaches on each of their slyly grinning faces, or sitting side by side sneaking licks from two oversized swirling colored lollipops *before* dinner.

Nick fashioned himself as BJ's watchful older brother early. He stood behind her swing on many spring days, pushing her as she laughed with delight in the white wooden swing that Bob nailed to a large oak tree. Nick recalls little of his long-ago bonding with BJ, but he does remember that swing.

"I didn't remember that scary time until I saw us in a picture, me standing behind BJ's swing. As I was pushing her, teaching her to pump her legs, she leaned back too far—or was it that she leaned the wrong way?—and fell out. Boy, did she scream and cry. Mom came flying out of the house. My heart was pumping like crazy, and I was trying to help BJ. Luckily the sounds coming out of my sister were a lot worse than anything else. She didn't get hurt, just messy from hitting the dirt."

During Nick's youngest years I didn't have the luxury of nurturing him hour by hour. I was a busy working mom. I needed Nick to help with the rest of the children. Because he was the oldest child in our family, Nick had a great deal of responsibility for his younger siblings. He was at the helm much of the time. Nicky never seemed to mind. Actually, he seemed especially well-suited for his caretaking jobs with BJ, Leslie, and tiny twins, Aaron and Angel.

Nick as Freddy Krueger Leading the Halloween Parade

Halloween has always been Nick's favorite holiday by far. As soon as we turned the page of our family calendar from September over to October, Nick wanted to consult with me about what he could dress up as for trick-or-treat time. Back in those years, we did not jump in the car and drive to a department store and browse through the aisles of ready-to-wear costumes and plastic masks that felt like jelly. We didn't have the money for store-bought costumes. Besides, Nick didn't need ready-to-wear when he had a crazy mother who could sew. His imagination coupled with my ability at the sewing machine and artsy flair fit the bill.

Nick imagined. I created. One year Nick's ideas turned him into Casper the Ghost. The costume was little more than a bedsheet, painted with a huge scarlet C on the front. One of the all-time best designs was our Dracula, Prince of Darkness. Not only was the black and white "suit" great, but the pasty white makeup and dark red lips made Nick perfectly vampire-ish. Nick and I really outdid ourselves that year. Another time, Nick wanted to be an Egyptian mummy. I took an old bedsheet and ripped it into pieces. I just kept on wrapping Nick up in the pieces until he did look as though he'd recently slipped out of a tomb.

The exact picture I want to bring to life now is

from the Halloween of 1988. At eight years old, Nick had his mind fixed on becoming Freddy Krueger. In the photo that officially stamps that day in our collective memory, Nick as Freddy stands next to BJ as a fairy princess. In front of Nick's Freddy-masked face he holds up a brown claw with silver-plated five-inch-long fingernails. His head is topped with a black fedora and he's wearing a modern red-and-black-striped Freddy shirt. Next to Nick's frightful sight, BJ is a vision of heaven wearing a long blond wig and a white dress with lots of golden jewelry around her neck and her waist. Her prop is a golden wand topped with a star covered with glow-in-the-dark sprinkles. Leslie, just two, is sucking her thumb—or is it the end of her pitchfork? Yes, Leslie was dressed up as a little red devil.

Nick led his sisters around quite often as a child, but he was never quite as excited as when he led them off on Halloween evening, teaching the youngest of his costumed brood the best ways to say "Trick or Treat."

> As it turns out Nick's monster fixation evolved into quite an award-winning concept. When Nick told me about his brainstorm that became the music video for "Everybody (Backstreet's Back)," it didn't surprise me. Nick as the Mummy, visions of Dracula, the Phantom of the Opera (not a Halloween costume but a role I dressed Nick for), all these characters had already made appearances at different points in Nick's childhood.

When Nick and the Backstreet Boys won MTV's Best Group Video award, and scenes from "Everybody" filled the screen, I could see Nicky on the eve of another Halloween extravaganza!

Nick with a Video Camera Filming a Sister Act

Our house had a piano, and that instrument served as the centerpiece for Nick to play maestro and later, Steven Spielberg. He would gather all the children around him. Sometimes they would play concert with my pint-sized combination of Leonard Bernstein and Raffi conducting this vocal ensemble in children's songs. As Nick grew and as more willing victims came along, the shows became more elaborate. Nick had an active—a mother might even say an overactive—imagination.

Nick's productions always started with an idea. The closet that held Bob's and my clothes became a favorite raiding place, where Nick would head to find "wardrobe." Among my dresses, shoes, and scarves, and Bob's boots, ties, and hats, Nick hunted for the perfect fashion ingredients to dress everyone up in dramatic design. The giggling that went on amid those makeovers, you wouldn't believe. Nick's cast, now dressed in character, would rehearse and perform.

Nick's father and I would get little handwritten invitations from the children to attend these seriously crafted performances. The Crayola-colored "playbill" would tell us exactly what time the curtain would go up. This was just one way that big brother ran his holding company. Sometimes it was skits, and sometimes musical shows.

Nick's shows were some dreamed-up version of the reruns he'd seen of the Ed Sullivan variety show. A favorite one looks as though Nick is directing a special on location in the exotic Hawaiian Islands.

Tropical fronds of palms are swaying right behind the star of this segment, Leslie. She is a brunette of around five years old, performing a big brother–choreographed hula dance. A genuine maize-colored grass skirt swishes back and forth across her hips. I have to adjust my eyes for a moment. The action looks so real I think I can see that grass skirt swing. Above it, Leslie's wearing a bathing suit decorated with pink Hawaiian leis and a tiara, commandeered from an old princess costume, no doubt.

The best touch in the picture is Nick standing off to the side filming the action with a video camera. Nick's dressed in a white T-shirt emblazoned with a big scary gray shark and the words "Shark Attack." He looks as if he can't decide whether he should be scenery or not. (Hollywood lore has it that this is how Steven Spielberg started.)

Those theatrical genes really stirred inside my Nick. Later when I actually enrolled him in real theatrical groups, it was a relief. At least he stayed out of my closet! If you've seen Nick with his blond hair standing on end, wearing orange glasses and a nerdy yellow boxed shirt, aiming a bow and arrow in the music video "As Long as You Love Me," you've seen vintage Nick. Give him a pile of silly clothes, and he's always loved creating an act.

Life's a Beach

Florida is a wonderful place to raise children. We lived close to many beaches. We have lots of family pictures of the days Nick and the rest of us spent on the beach, scavenging for beach glass or picking up shells.

There's Nick, a wet and sandy five-year-old in navy-blue bathing trunks, bending down to feed crackers to five hungry seagulls. On the next page of a family album, a twelve-year-old Nick and his sister BJ smile like the king and queen of the hill, a big sandy hill. They are sitting in the sand, leaning on a hill they have built. In the middle of that hill is my head. My two oldest have buried me in sand up to my neck. All you can see are the tips of my toes at the other end of the sandy tomb and their ear-to-ear grins.

We have underwater photos of Nick scuba diving. We are a scuba-certified family. We had friends down from New York last summer. Their fourteen-year-old daughter, who wants to be a marine biologist, got into a conversation with Nick about sharks. As she said, "I love sharks," Nick replied, "I caught a black-tipped shark out back off our dock." Then the hair on the back of his neck surely started to stand up.

"I'm scared of sharks," he confessed. "I have a fear of staying on top of the water. I've heard too many horror stories about sailors jumping ship and getting eaten in the middle of the ocean by predatory sharks. I'm personally fine when I get down under the water in my scuba stuff, but floating up top, that's not for me!"

Looking at this scuba shot, it occurs to me that Nick and the rest of us haven't had enough time lately to enjoy the Florida sunshine or the ocean . . . with or without sharks.

Sometimes It Rains Cats and Dogs

I've taught Nick and his brother and sisters that their place in the family is special, and their contributions are essential. Nick was the first one to learn to live this Carter ideal. He was a big help. My children all love and value one another.

I confess that Nick pushed himself into this part of our story, along with BJ. Aaron and Angel wanted to stick in a few cents, too, but the twins couldn't get a word in edgewise. When Nick and BJ reviewed how I describe our perfect little Carter family life, they told me I left out some of the truth. Okay, okay. It's true.

Nick: "BJ and I got along fine. *And we fought like cats and dogs!* How could you forget that, Mom? In Tampa our bedrooms were straight across from each other, and we fought so bad."

BJ: "Nick, you used to throw action figures at me. I got you into trouble more often."

Nick: "Yeah, you always got me into trouble, and that made me so mad."

Now Nick's temperature was beginning to rise. Uh-oh, I do remember this.

BJ (starting to raise her voice to a feverish pitch): "You *always* started it!"

Nick (giving back in an equally emotional pitch): "I did not always *start it!* Dad would give in because you were a lot smaller than me. And you'd whine, 'He started it.' Dad would tell me to go to my room when I didn't *do* anything. You always blamed me."

BJ (still chiming in and trying to outyell Nick): "You did so. You picked on me. You called me names."

I raised my hands in exasperation the way I used to when these two were much smaller. Just like old times, the squabbling temporarily stopped. Calm began to settle between them again.

BJ apologetically offered, "Sometimes I admit I did get you into trouble when it wasn't your fault."

So there you have it. A normal slice of life. BJ and Nick and I will tell one last story about brotherly love. We remembered this one as we looked at pictures of the home we live in now. At first sight, this house created a lot of problems . . . for one of us.

This incident happened when Nick was fourteen and BJ had turned twelve. It was time to move from our Tampa home. Upon hearing about the house and the move, BJ said, "Move? I don't want to move! If you sell this house, I'll never come out of my bedroom." With those highly emotional and fighting words, BJ crawled under her bed and refused to come out.

Nick tried to reason with her, telling her that we'd been in this home for seven years and we were all cramped in it. We needed more space, he said, so it was time to move on. Nothing he tried calmed her down. So, an exasperated and yet sympathetic big brother got down on his hands and knees, reached under the bed, grabbed her feet with his hands, and started pulling her out.

"BJ," he said as she struggled, "everything is going to be fine."

BJ relented then, listening to her big brother as she always had. I hope she always will.

As the oldest sibling, Nick always played a prominent role in keeping close the relationships between the children. Nick's brother and sisters are very special to him, and it goes both ways. Our pictures say as much. Because of this special bond, our family not only lives in harmony but we are able to work together toward achieving what we all want out of life.

7

Auditioning for Mom . . . A Legendary Debut

Nick has had a longtime love affair with the lens of a camera, any kind of a camera—still, film, or video. He treats it as if it's a partner in an intimate conversation. When photographed, something magical about him comes through. Sometimes he sends out a pure emotion such as innocence or arrogance, or he merely exudes a compelling presence. In one pose Nick may look guileless with the wide smile of the boy next door. In another, he may smirk like the cat that swallowed the canary. Or Nick, scowling, may seem the quintessential teen rebel—just the sort a mother does not want picking up her daughter for a date! Nick in print or on video charms, seduces, and even hypnotizes. I think that's fair to say even if he is my own flesh and blood.

Nick first seduced and was seduced by the camera

in 1988. It was around Christmastime that year when we purchased our first family video camera. Like many other parents, Bob and I wanted to get footage of Nick, BJ, Leslie, Angel, and Aaron while they were young. We wanted to capture our own private collection of emotionally moving moments and quiet times, as well as the frantic escapades of the Carter clan.

Celluloid memories become priceless as time goes on. All parents feel that way whether their children grow into superstars or not. Bob and I sensed that our children were growing up so fast that we had to rush to preserve images of them.

From the start Nick's interest in the video camera outdid our enthusiasm. He tried incessantly to get in front of the camera. Regardless of who we were focusing the camcorder on, Nick chimed in with a song or interrupted with a narrator's voice-over. Roll 'em! Action! As we filmed our children opening their Christmas presents—Nick was eight years old, BJ, six, and Leslie, about two at the time—Nick popped up, saying *"Hi! It's me, Nick!"* We panned one of our girls frolicking around the house. All of a sudden, Nick poked his head into the frame, chattering away.

One particularly hilarious home movie deserves the title *In Search of.* . . . Leslie is hunting for her baby bottle. Nick is the Leonard Nimoy–type narrator. His entertaining buttinsky commentary on his sister's travails made us laugh. Another filmstrip standout resembles *Rescue 911.* My girls look for trouble, and Nick, as serious as William Shatner, analyzes their mischief. I started to realize with some ambivalence that Nick exhibited the characteristics of—what shall I call it?—a kid with a showbiz personality.

It amuses and delights us to look at those old videos now. We played them again recently and we laughed until it hurt. Back then, though, I didn't laugh all that much. I have to be honest and admit that at first I worried. When I realized just how desperately Nick wanted to be the center of attention in these home video sessions, I became concerned. I began to ask myself, *Was Nick starved for attention?*

In our large family, many things happened *all* the time and *all at once*. Nick craved the limelight. What did that mean? At a loss for an answer, I didn't know what to do about my pint-sized attention-seeker. I imagined a future in which Nick bore psychological scars from being neglected. Had I raised a guy destined to search interminably for attention or perhaps for approval? Did Nick's personality sentence him to an eternal battle for recognition? I worked myself into quite a state over Nick's recurring shenanigans to get noticed.

I made it a point then to tuck Nick in and linger for a few minutes to talk with him about his day. I tried to give him an opportunity, an opening to tell me if he felt neglected or to confide any problems on his mind. He never expressed any worries or difficulties at those good-night kiss rituals. He seemed carefree, happy. Then later, lying in bed next to my husband, I heard an imaginary worrywart on the other side of me whispering in my ear: *Is Nick all right?* As much to silence that nagging ghost as to shake off my doubts, I talked about it with Bob.

We thought that surely our large and busy household had something to do with it. I ran a time-consuming nursing home care facility. I took the emotional temperatures of our older residents as well as monitoring their health. One of them often needed a moment of kindness. Or another asked for a little extra time to tell me a story about a daughter or a grandchild who lived far away.

In between I often found myself taking one of my own little girls' temperatures, investigating a cranky mood. Grocery shopping, planning and preparing meals, handling correspondence for my elderly patients, doing the monthly bills, filling my calendar with dates for "meet the teacher night" and pediatrician or dentist appointments—my days always came scheduled with a killer list of things to do. To be heard above the roar of our bustling everyday lives, Nick had to assert himself loudly and clearly.

So that's why he acted like a clown or some kind of ham, I told myself. What was so unusual about a boy of eight wanting to be the big cheese in the family? Nick *was* the oldest. I rationalized his "ham and big cheese" behavior during my midnight soul searching. I told myself that all kids are not equal, that some always seem to require more—more time, more love, more feedback than others. Perhaps a child who needed more described my Nicky. That line of reasoning explained why he always sought out center stage.

Looking back, I recognize that Nick's antics and attempts to steal the limelight from his sisters were characteristic of a born entertainer. Nicky's cutting up on camera served as dress rehearsals. He liked emoting. *Hi! It's me, Nick!* He loved to mimic the baritone seriousness of the newsman. The music inside him simply burst into song. His energy spilled out in the form of jokes or silly commentary.

With the wisdom of hindsight, I see that labeling Nick's behavior "acting out" was incorrect. Drawing conclusions about his feeling neglected missed the mark. Nick didn't misbehave. I understand now that Nick's craving for the spotlight, his incredible drive, and relentless energy are responsible for Nick's success at a young age. Back then, though, figuring all this out and deciding whether I should be doing more for Nick haunted me.

Mom, This One's for You!

Some days I looked around the house for Nick and couldn't find him. When I peeked outside into our backyard, though, I'd often spot Nick bouncing on our trampoline and singing. He directed this impromptu performance at other children peering at him over the picket fence. Laughing out loud, I'd think, *What a character Nick is!*

Other boys played cowboys and Indians, or cops and robbers. Neighboring children picked up dolls and carriages, imitating their parents with a game of house. Nick would play some of the usual childhood games that boys play, war of some sort, or the usual gunfights. Yet I have to say in looking back at Nick, he preferred the make-believe game that would have to be simply called "star and audience." Nick always headlined, singing an operetta or performing acrobatic feats.

Many an afternoon, I stumbled upon Nick singing to no one. No giggling children dangled on the other side of the neighboring fence. I asked once whom he was singing to.

"My audience today is the blades of grass, Mom," Nick replied. No hint of embarrassment or self-consciousness showed in his response, only a distinct twinkle in his eye. Fantasy concerts and playground performances totally occupied Nick's attention.

For me, the pieces of Nick's theatrical personality fell into place slowly. I added up my video hog monopolizing the spotlight with my backyard Pavarotti. Nick was deep inside his own special game of monopoly, but not the classic Milton Bradley board game. He didn't plot and plan to buy real estate or hotels. Nick was bent on acquiring an audience. He dreamed of Broadways. Instead of wanting to collect rents or salaries from the other players, Nick pursued proving his talents, getting acclaim and fame. Being a child, Nick's star search initially had goals aimed at next-door audiences.

One day, I completely understood my son's talent. This is a time I recall clearly as a turning point. I knew, without a doubt, that great things lay ahead for Nick.

Many stories bounce around out there in the teen magazine scene, and over the electronic highway, telling how Nick started singing. Some are partly true. Some are downright false. Being his mother and having watched his singing career begin, I can tell you the truth.

Music always played in our house. The radio blared or murmured in the background virtually all the time. Bob and I exposed Nick to a variety of music. Being partial to the sounds of our youth, we liked the "oldies" stations.

As a girl, I recall many nights when I slipped out our front door and inside the family car. I turned on the old radio, and listened to Casey Kasem count down the top one hundred songs. Songs from your adolescence stay with you, always. Years from now today's Backstreet Boys hits will be the "oldies" of scores of current fans.

About this time, rap invaded the music scene. Bob and I remained loyal to our tastes and rejected it. We preferred music with strong vocal performances. Those kinds of songs became the sound track of Nick's childhood. Ever the ham around the house, Nick, our very own little musical Pied Piper, led the children hither and yon, around the backyard, playwriting, playacting, and dancing to our music.

Nick's dad had a habit of cutting down trees all the time with his chain saw. On certain days I wondered if my husband could have been a beaver in a past life. Several unattractive tree stumps littered the backyard as a result.

I favored one stump in particular near the pool for sunning and teaching the children to swim. I spent all my spare time there. One afternoon, Simon and Garfunkel's "Bridge Over Troubled Water" caught the breeze and coasted across the yard as the hot summer sun beat down.

That song was special during my childhood. My father had been a huge fan of Simon and Garfunkel during the '60s and '70s, when they ruled the pop charts. They topped his list of favorite artists. Twice during those years they performed in our Chautauqua area. I learned to strum the guitar a bit around that time. My dad played and taught me a few chords. I stretched my fingers across the fret of my guitar, experimenting until I found the right sounds, and fleshed out those songs over and over. I sang them until I knew all the Simon and Garfunkel lyrics by heart.

I told Nick that I just loved "Bridge Over Troubled Water." In a heartfelt way he told me he did too.

I remember feeling pleased that he appreciated the kind of music I liked. What I call *real music* is music with a moving melody and a passion that lasts forever. The artist who sings *real music* must take a song and infuse it with feeling, using no less than all of his body and soul.

I remember telling Nick, "Honey, if you could sing like that, you'd be a superstar."

Later on, I happened to go out and buy that tape. I never saw Nick reach for it. He must have picked it up, though, and learned it on his own.

A few days later, I stood at the sink in our kitchen, washing the breakfast dishes. The window was open, and I heard music. I stopped, turned off the faucet, wiped my hands on a dish towel, and went over to the window. I glanced out to find the source of the sounds filtering in.

The voice was strong and beautiful. It had perfect pitch. As I looked out, I saw Nick. He sat in our backyard, perched on one of those tree stumps, singing. He treated me to the most stirring version of "Bridge Over Troubled Water" that I had ever heard. My nine-year-old son passionately performed and blew Art Garfunkel right out of the water!

I dropped everything. I listened with true joy in my heart.

Nick saw me. Obviously, he had planned this. He watched as I beamed proudly the whole time he sang. When he finished holding the last note, I applauded ecstatically. I had tears in my eyes. I saw the tears forming in the corners of his blue eyes as well. When I hugged Nick and pressed his face against my cheek, our tears of happiness and mutual understanding mingled. Right then and there I took my son's talent seriously. Nick was still a child, but he intended to tell me something with his premeditated performance. I received the full weight of his desire that morning. After praising and congratulating Nick, I rushed into the house to find Bob.

"Bob," I shouted, beside myself with excitement. "I just heard Nick singing 'Bridge Over Troubled Water' out in the backyard. His voice is unbelievable! I've just got to do something about it."

Our tears joined together on behalf of Nick's destiny. My son needed my help to get him on the right road to find his way.

I ran for the phone book to find a vocal teacher. I didn't know it at the time, but my reaction and the actions that fol-

At the age of nine, Nick had a voice and an ambition, both older than his years, to perform before an audience. I went out to find him his audience.

lowed changed Nick's future, and our whole family's as well. Nick's solo rendition that summer morning created a bridge out of sounds that carried us from one life into another, where dreams became everyday realities.

At Nick's defining moment on that tree stump, he had an audience of one, me. After that, day by day, year by year, that cheering squad multiplied. When Nick sang for teachers and coaches, talent agents and dance studio owners, and then television workshop producers, he won them over one by one, one song at a time.

Now, at eighteen, Nick croons '90s style, sometimes with a whine, a whisper, or a rousing wallop. He swivels and slides into slick choreography, never missing a beat, and flashes the smile that's inspired a million girls to have a crush on him. He seems to do all this effortlessly, as naturally as he breathes. In his white satin suit, he is such a professional. Nick's spontaneous charm and talent alone wouldn't make him the performer he is today, if he weren't a professional.

What does that mean? Well, the music video "All I Have to Give" opens with the camera moving in close to capture Nick's face. He begins singing, softly, sincerely and almost grudgingly. As he sings the word "smile" he looks up, straight into the camera, and his lips curve into a perfect smile, as if right on cue. Now that's professional!

I was so impressed that I even commented on it. I asked Nick, "How did you manage to transform your expression so subtly, so seamlessly, exactly in sync with the lyrics you were singing?"

Nick smiled. He never quite gave me a straight answer. I could tell he appreciated my compliment, though. Sometimes Nicky and I understand one another perfectly, without saying a word, and I'm sure he realized I'd know the answer, when I got over being wowed and stopped to think about it. It was the product of Nick's talented inspiration coupled with training and practice. That's professionalism . . . and the first step toward it was taken in our backyard.

8

School Days, ☆ Audition Afternoons, ☆ and Theatrical Nights

Auditioning for the mother who loves you in the security of your own backyard is one thing. Strutting your vocal stuff for a total stranger is quite another. Nick always had that certain courage that is essential for those who want to perform. He always exuded confidence even if, at the beginning, it mingled with stage fright. To this day, I've never seen Nick question his talent or try to second-guess his creative instincts. He has always had *it*. On some level, even as a young boy, Nick knew—he believed in himself, probably even before his father and I did. Once Nick convinced me, though, I backed him up one hundred percent.

Nick's talent was raw, but wonderful and perfectly obvious . . . to me. I knew that vocal lessons were the way to improve upon his gift, but I knew less about how to make this happen. I took the first logical step—I let my fingers do the walking through the Yellow Pages. I decided to look under "Music," then I came to a section called "Music Instruction" with a subheading, "Vocal Instruction." I found the name of June Daniels, whom I called.

Ms. Daniels told me that she had never taken a nine-year-old student before. However, she agreed to audition Nick, saying that after she had the opportunity to hear him she would decide whether to make an exception. The "or not" dangled in the silence after she spoke. That spelled P-R-E-S-S-U-R-E. In anticipation, Nick worked on perfecting his rendition of "Bridge Over Troubled Water."

The day we arrived for the audition, Nick acted nervous. I recognized the vibrations because his trembling was in sync with mine. To our surprise, June Daniels turned out to be a much older woman than we had assumed. She was somewhere in her early sixties. She had pep and vitality, and moved with an ageless grace; her personality lit up the room. She greeted us warmly, but in a dignified fashion. She had jet-black hair swooped up into a huge beehive that looked to me like cotton candy made of licorice. Lots and lots of makeup colored her face and was a tip-off that she had more than a passing knowledge of the theater's footlights. She explained to us that she acted as well as sang herself and performed regularly in the Spanish Lyric Acting Group, a Tampa community theater troupe.

I introduced myself and Nick. As I looked around

the room, I noticed that the walls held theatrical memorabilia. Photographs of famous actors in plays returned my stare. Several stills captured June Daniels in her younger years. Having grown up around my acting-buff dad, I felt an instant rapport with her. I looked at Nick and indicated the dramatic accessories and characters that decorated the room. Nick's gaze followed mine. He, too, instantly felt more at home. I saw him exhale, relieved by his surroundings. A beautiful grand piano stood in the center of the room . . . waiting.

I told June Daniels outright that I thought my nine-year-old son had a gift. Call it woman's intuition combined with a mother's protective instinct, but I felt she was highly skeptical. Would this episode end in a big disappointment for Nick? Mentally, I crossed my fingers and my toes. I knew how seriously my son took this tryout. I held my breath, trying to stifle any trace of doubt from slipping into the atmosphere.

Nick began to sing "Bridge Over Troubled Water."

As the melody crescendoed, Nick and his voice soared above the butterflies that I knew fluttered inside him. Silently, my whole being said *Yes*! Nick was delivering—not only perfect pitch but also passion. He was passing the first test of his talent with flying colors. He was right to be doing this. If I had had any doubts, Nick sang them away. I looked at June, wondering if she was as impressed as I. The expression on her face, her twinkling smile, told me she was impressed, all right. Very impressed. Enthusiastically and in the wink of an eye, June Daniels agreed to take Nick on as a student. Now I had a valued, professional opinion. Within days Nick and I began weekly drives to her home for lessons that lasted half an hour.

June, whose creative reference point was musical theater, encouraged Nick to learn songs from musicals. From *Mary Poppins,* she chose "Supercalifragilisticexpialidocious," "Feed the Birds" and "Let's Go Fly a Kite." These were a few of those first songs that she and Nick worked on. As Nick spit out that mouthful of staccato, tongue-twisting "Supercalifragilistic" lyrics, the line about sounding "precocious" described him to a T. He had a big voice for such a little boy.

June took great care in teaching Nick more than phrasing a lyric. She taught him little theatrical gestures to accompany his singing, for instance how to move and what to do with his hands. June stood right next to Nick and showed him how to use his body to emphasize a song, or enhance an emotion that he needed to get across with his singing.

When Nick sang about flying a kite, high in the sky, he looked up. The upward glance was part gesture, practiced as June instructed. Yet, I knew it was more. When Nick raised his eyes, he saw what I did up there, a piece of the sky holding a special star waiting to be inscribed with his name. Both of us knew there was a long way to go . . . and a lot of work to be done to connect celestial dots until he reached that special star.

Nick stood erect by June's piano, the posture she prescribed. He did exactly what his vocal coach told him to do. I attended every lesson along with Nick. Afterward, at home, I reinforced his vocal teacher's instructions, often using tapes made during lessons, and he practiced all week to master a song. Nick was an excellent little student. This surprised and delighted June.

Nick and I have often reminisced about her and how lucky we were to find her. It was a stroke of good fortune to have someone as nurturing and able as June Daniels for his first vocal teacher.

Looking for a Pond, Swimming with the Sharks

I turned to June for some direction. I inquired: How do I get Nick the opportunity to perform on a real stage for a live group of listeners? June advised me to watch the local newspapers for news of auditions for theatrical productions and talent shows. I began scanning *The Tampa Tribune* for those kinds of announcements.

Before this, I hadn't paid much attention to the local arts scene. Once I did, however, I began to realize just how fertile the ground was for creative people in the Tampa Bay area. One of the few communities in Florida that really gave the arts a priority, Tampa resembled the cultural community of Chautauqua in upstate New York where I grew up.

Primarily because of Disney World and Nickelodeon, many show business opportunities arose. Tampa's aspiring young singers, actors, and dancers had chances galore. The bright side promised the opportunity to be discovered. The dark side was a land filled with petty jealousies and sneaky enemies. Nick and I stepped into a highly competitive child-star marketplace. To call it a real soap opera entitled *The Young and the Heartless* is not an exaggeration.

I read the news of a talent show open to all ages and all types of entertainers—singers, dancers, impressionists, comedians—being held at the Royalty Theater in Clearwater. Nick and I eagerly decided to give it a try. June agreed to accompany Nick on piano on his best song, "Let's Go Fly a Kite." Neither Nick nor I comprehended the jungle that we innocently and naively walked into.

This was Nick's very first performance before an audience of strangers. When he walked out on that stage the first time, I thought I could see his little knees shaking. My knees started to shake, too, because I knew how much this meant to Nick. June began to play the introduction on the piano. When Nick started singing, a hush fell over the crowd.

I have trouble remembering that first performance because I was so keyed up while Nick sang. My hands trembled so with excitement that I had to wrestle those jitters in order to keep the video camera steady—which of course I'd brought along! I do remember knowing that Nick's voice sounded amazingly loud. After he sang the last note, he took a little bow. Dead silence, for what seemed like an eternity, followed. I must have perceived the moment as if in some kind of mental slow motion. Then the audience burst into applause. I was so proud that I felt as if I would burst.

That applause said it all. A new entertainer had just entered the scene. I will never forget the look on Nick's face. It broadcast that Nick not only loved to sing, he loved to perform for a live audience. The applause delivered something that only a performer can truly explain. If I listed Nick's favorite sounds, applause is right up there with the sound of the ocean and the beat of a drum. From that day forward, Nick and I searched for places where he could perform and once again enjoy the sound of applause.

Our adventure was an uphill climb. We traveled to singing lessons and auditions, juggling Nick's school schedule, and battling for those prized opportunities. Not only did we have to manage all that, but we had to keep adding to Nick's professional portfolio.

Nick auditioned for a part in *Annie Get Your Gun*. The director took me aside and confidentially counseled me. He said, "Your son needs to learn how to dance. He'll lose a lot of roles if he can't dance." Like this one. He went on to tell me that Nick's fine singing qualified him—but the part called for him to dance, so he had to choose someone else. He picked Nick for the chorus.

Naturally, Nick and I felt disappointed. The *Annie Get Your Gun* episode identified for us a real stumbling block. Nick and I both knew that his dancing was stiff and awkward. Did we see the director's criticism as a put-down? No. Quite the contrary, we agreed that it was valid and we should act accordingly. Nick said that he wanted to learn to dance. With my can-do attitude, I concentrated on finding him a good dance studio.

At a yard sale I met Elaine Howard, a neighbor, who ran a dance troupe called Jackie's Juniors in which her daughter, Starla, danced. I told Elaine all about Nick. Once she heard and saw him, Elaine knew Nick would be an asset. I thought, here is a chance for Nick to learn jazz and tap. We began driving twice a week to Jackie's studio.

Elaine booked Jackie's Juniors featuring Nick singing "God Bless the USA" at the grand opening of the Tampa Convention Center. A local radio DJ interviewed Nick, complimenting him by saying, "You really knocked my socks off." Nick, inexperienced in the ways of the media, blurted out, "I bet I knocked a lot of people's socks off." Now it was time for modesty lessons, too. Nick had a crush on Starla but, alas, he didn't knock her socks off.

I learned as we went along. The child who had the best odds for success was the one who could sing, dance, *and* act. I saw to it that Nick developed into what is known in show business circles as "a triple threat." I think my most important role, though, was as the emotional accompanist. Just as Nick needed June Daniels at first to accompany his vocals on the piano, my son needed me to act as his nurturer, cheerleader, and buffer.

As we went from audition to audition, we ran up against a breed of stage mothers the likes of which I hadn't imagined. They behaved ruthlessly. And even worse, they taught their children to be cunning, too. They greeted my child, or someone else's, with remarks like "New haircut! You should have waited until tomorrow!" or "What happened to your shoes? Too bad you can't afford a better pair!" These calculated, well-rehearsed barrages were aimed at throwing off the other child's concentration, or annihilating self-confidence the very moment before auditioning.

These perfectly timed digs derailed and deflated many youngsters. I saw it happen. I hadn't prepared Nick for this kind of sophisticated brutality. I took the opposite tack because, after all, he was still a child. I encouraged Nick to relax and have fun. I told him to go ahead and try to make friends. Nick made friends easily. On this circuit of auditions for musicals, and for bit parts in television and film, Nick ran into two boys again and again. He struck up an acquaintance with AJ McLean and Howie Dorough. Along with Nick they eventually became three fifths of the Backstreet Boys.

I'm not naive. And the more I saw what was going on, the more I realized I had to prepare Nick for what could happen before, during, and after the rounds of singing, dancing, and reading lines. I had to arm my son for survival in this creative jungle. I intended to see to it that Nick was not undone.

I still remember a little girl and her mother. She

and Nick both auditioned for a plum television role in a new series. It became crystal clear to Nick and me that this child had been taught not to chitchat, not to be friendly. She behaved in a very standoffish way. Nick tried to make conversation. In return he got the brush-off.

The girl's mother drove a luxury car with a vanity license plate that referred to her child. She intimidated me (and surely every other parent who crossed her path) with her ice-queen silence, her sleek good looks, and her expensively dressed figure. She stared past Nick and me, treating us both as if we didn't exist. With her cold shoulder and expressionless face, she intentionally conveyed her message that we didn't belong in the same audition as her daughter.

Nick ran up against this duo four times, vying for that unisex role. I wish that nice folks finished first here, but in this case that didn't happen. Nick lost out to the child. Yet Nick and I walked away from that experience having learned a valuable lesson about how not to act and how not to treat people. Stage mothers like that woman, and prima donnas like her child, inspired me—in reverse! I set my mind to *never* act like that, ever! I pledged to never let my son try to make people feel invisible.

As it turned out, Nick's future proved to have the better ending in both the short term and the long run. The series got canceled shortly after it went on the air.

Throughout such ordeals testing character as well as talent, I encouraged Nick to be himself. Nick and I spent a lot of time driving to and from lessons and rehearsals. Nick did his homework in the car. We used the private time, the one-on-one stretches in an otherwise crowded family life, to catch up with each other. During these special moments, I gave Nick my advice. I guided him on how to run the child-star gauntlet.

"You just worry about Nick" was my title and recurring theme. I gave Nick lessons on what to watch out for and how to handle potential problems.

Nick heard the following guidelines from me repeatedly:

- Don't listen to what other people say.
- Don't be influenced by what they do.
- What anyone else says won't affect you, as long as you know what you want and who you are.
- Be sure of yourself.
- Be true to yourself.
- Go for it.
- You just worry about Nick, no one else, and you'll do fine.

Superkid . . . a Quick-Change Artist

Most of these auditions and the performances that Nick gave happened after school. After a night of performing, did Nick wake up tired? Did I have to drag him out of bed and nag him to hurry up and get ready for school? Didn't he complain about being under a lot of pressure? Did he have trouble combining studying for that science test with having to learn lines for a reading?

The truth of the matter is that Nick always had and still has bundles of energy. This multidimensional life never posed a conflict. Nick liked his life, enjoyed the excitement and the diversion. He is blessed with the most active imagination I have ever encountered. He has one of those hyper-creative personalities. The next rehearsal or audition energized him. The challenge I, as his mother, found most difficult? How to keep all that energy focused!

I made certain that I always talked to Nick's teachers about his aspirations in the theater and the after-school activities that Nick was engaged in. Most of them were supportive and cooperated with any scheduling problems. One of them in particular stands out. This teacher apparently had a special place in her heart for an artistic, creative student like my son. Nick's fourth-grade teacher, Ms. Montes de Oca, allowed Nick to capitalize on his talents, casting him as the lead in *Phantom of the Opera*. She took Nick under her wing. Last year Nick decided to remind her of that.

When the Backstreet Boys, successful in Europe but as yet unrecognized in America, scheduled their first big concert in Tampa, Nick insisted I telephone Ms. Montes de Oca. After I spoke to her, Nick took the phone.

"Remember me?" he said to his fourth-grade teacher.

"Of course I do, Nick," she told him. "I've been following your career."

Nick invited her to be his special guest at that event. How rewarding for me to see that Nick learned a lesson that I tried hard to teach him. Acknowledge those people who helped you. Remember them. Thank them. Nick did.

Even Small-Town Fame Had a Price, and Nick Paid

I don't want to leave the impression that Nick's preteen, star-climbing life lacked trouble. Throughout middle school, Nick played a junior version of Superman. During the school day, he took on the role of Clark Kent. He tried to be a regular kid, and to keep a low profile. He didn't talk about his "other life." Why risk arousing feelings of jealousy with tales of singing in musicals or acting in plays? On this we both agreed. Nick accepted the fact that he had to handle his schoolwork well and, for the most part, he did.

Once the school bell rang, off Nick went into that "telephone booth." He changed into his star "costume." Out of his backpack, he pulled the script for the week. Taking a last look in the mirror, he primed his confidence. He tuned up his singing voice, and put on his dancing (or acting) shoes. (Could Nick's quick-change superkid history explain why he has drawn and written a comic book? In it, he and his Backstreet brothers morph into superheroes bent on saving the world.)

I didn't know it then, but when Nick attended Young Junior High School, his peers teased him, apparently a great deal. Bullies baited and threatened Nick, and girls—yes, even the girls!—shunned him. Nick never expressed any of this to me, in any way. So you can imagine my surprise when I heard Nick, now an eighteen-year-old, tell me the truth about middle school. Nick wanted me to include the following intimate, candid confession in these pages. He sat down and looked me straight in the eye and told me what he wanted people to know.

"There's a side of me that nobody knows because I never tell anybody," Nick began. His eyes looked down and his voice grew soft. The expression in those soulful eyes showed pain at what he was about to explain. I also saw a kind of silent apology for not telling me, his mother, any of this years ago.

"In school I was a nerd," Nick continued. "I was one of those kids who walked down the hallways always with his head down. I never wanted to get involved in conversation. I wasn't very personable."

I must have appeared to be an awfully glum audience, because Nick joked, "That's changed, as you can tell." But as I grinned to echo his smile, Nick got back to his serious tone as he went on, "I was shy. Since I was so into the acting and singing, you took me out of school earlier than the others a lot so we could do things. The other boys didn't understand that. They hated me for getting time off from school. In their eyes, I wasn't one of them.

"I was teased. There were even fights. Honestly, if

I had not had this constructive avenue to walk into with my singing and all, I think I might have taken a different route. It might not have been a good route, either. I could have turned out differently. My whole life would have been different. That's why I encourage the young kids I meet all around the world to stay away from drugs and to find something constructive to do with their lives. I know how it feels to go through your teenage years feeling bad and looking for a way to feel better about yourself."

This conversation made me concerned that I had been a lax mother. How could I have missed the painful experiences that Nick lived through? Why didn't I see the signs?

I didn't pick up any of this because Nick was careful to hide the clues. Like all young adolescent boys, he didn't tell his mother everything. Being ridiculed because he danced, because he acted, because he got out of school early to go to callbacks was humiliating. Boys don't want to portray these kinds of episodes for fear that their mothers will see them as foolish and weak, too. Later I asked BJ about this. She knew. She actually saw Nick suffer at the hands of obnoxious, jealous boys and girls on occasions. She and Nick kept all that private, part of a close pact that has always existed between the two of them.

It wasn't fair but it was fact. Because Nick's life didn't resemble the ones his peers lived, he suffered at their hands. Nick didn't dribble a basketball, dodge the defenders, dance around the defense until he got a clear shot. He didn't huddle on the junior varsity football field, order the play, or steamroll through a line of hefty fullbacks. He didn't kick the soccer ball upfield with fancy footwork, waiting for the moment to whack it precisely into the net. Nick didn't play sports in school. He did, absolutely, take part in a highly competitive game.

He aimed for the brass ring, not a hoop or a net. He calculated his moves, assessed his talented rivals, and kept his eye on the goal. He tackled competition head-on. Nick practiced and developed fancy footwork and his inner game. He worked as hard as any middle school athlete to make sure that his performances scored. I coached him all the way with as much fire as any gym teacher.

Managing an aspiring child star is demanding work. It is also expensive, especially for a family without extra cash to burn. There were voice lessons, dance lessons, traveling back and forth in a car with an insatiable thirst for more gasoline and oil. I set my determined mind to do it, regardless of the cost. Bob and I put Nick's blossoming career above all. We paid a price. The Carters didn't go to the movies very often. We ate a diet that consisted mainly of spaghetti, goulash, and macaroni and cheese. All of us did whatever was necessary to pay for what Nick needed. Nick and I, and our family, had a goal and sacrifice went along with it.

Our nourishment came from watching Nick blossom as he performed in a wide range of musical productions, children's television programs, and talent shows.

9

Climbing the Stairway to Stardom

During the hustle and bustle of Nick's showbiz beginnings, I didn't recognize the emotional scars of those school yard confrontations. When I picked Nick up at school, he always seemed happy or at least to be enthusiastic about what lay ahead for the afternoon. If Nick didn't seem to have a horde of friends from the local middle school skidding into our driveway, it didn't strike me as a problem. He made so many friends among other performers and his afterschool activities always seemed more like play for him than work.

In addition to the youngsters, both older and younger, that Nick grew close to, he struck up relationships with a number of adults who played instrumental roles in moving him along toward his dream. Nick had wonderful mentors, people who helped him develop.

Mentors don't wear a sign on their lapel that says, "Hey, listen to me, kid. I can help you!" Mentors come in all shapes and sizes. Furthermore, they can pop up in the most unlikely places. Where would I have been without the invaluable guidance of Jan, the heavyset, older, blond woman, whose favorite place just happened to be a barstool at The Centerfold Lounge? It was she who helped me change careers.

Nick always had supporters within our family. I've mentioned how Nick's great-grandfather Robert Neal taught Nick when he was little. Years afterwards when Nick was ten, Nick sang "Amazing Grace" with my father at a church service at the Hall of Christ and in the Hall of Philosophy at the renowned Chautauqua Institution, the same place where I married Nick's father. I still get chills up and down my spine when I recall that performance.

Nick got on easily with adults who held out a helping hand. There are a few faces in particular that I see as I look through Nick's first playbills and the first set of newspaper clippings about him. These were the men and women who were responsible for Nick's early opportunities on the stage, in television productions, print, and film.

Nick on the World Stage . . . in a Way

Nick auditioned for director Rick D'Onofrio, who ran a theater company called Stages Productions in St. Petersburg. Rick and his wife, Terri, had been educated in theater arts at Valdosta State University in

Georgia. Their goal was to bring more theatrical events to Tampa. At first Nick tried out for a part in a production called *The Littlest Angel*. Judged not quite experienced enough, Nick only made it into the chorus.

However, Rick saw something special in Nick. He was the kind of person who found working with children very rewarding. He recognized Nick's enthusiasm and how he listened and how he worked to get better. Here, he said, was a boy with more than the usual amount of talent and dedication. So this director took Nick under his wing and began to give Nick instruction in the art of live theater.

Nick landed a lead role in another D'Onofrio project, *Peter and the Wolf*. It opened at the Tampa Bay Performing Arts Center. Then the production toured schools throughout our area. *Peter and the Wolf* is a complicated play to pull off. Nick performed superbly. The only child in the ensemble, he impressed the director, the cast, and his audience.

I used to bring demos (demonstration recordings) that Nick made at ten years old for the cast of *Peter and the Wolf* to listen to. Nick recorded the songs in a local studio with a music machine. That was my son's first studio experience! Nick sang vocals from the rock group Journey's album on which his favorite song was Steve Perry's classic masterpiece, "Lights." Nick has performed that song as a Backstreet Boy. (What a thrill it would be for Nick to record that song someday with Steve Perry, his early rock'n'roll inspiration.)

I told everyone, "Nick is going to be a famous singer someday." They all said, "Sure." As community theater veterans, many of them undoubtedly had aspirations like Nick's at one time. Success hadn't happened for them, and they became jaded. When they expressed skepticism, I rolled out my defenses, and tuned out their cynical words. I made sure that neither Nick nor I became infected with that kind of disillusionment. Staying positive remained my motto. Our gait called for head up, eyes fixed always on the finish line—that star.

Nick did so well that Rick wrote a musical with Nick in mind—*Holidays Around the World,* a musical and dance revue.

Nick wore a Bart Simpson T-shirt, dressing the part of a smart-talking bad boy. Nick leads the audience on a humorous tour around the globe. The show portrayed the cultural holiday customs of each country in song and dance. Nick's lines expressed that Simpson mouthiness and a hint of high jinks even as his character learns the true meaning of the holiday. Nick, and Santa on a unicycle, visit Jamaica, Israel, the Soviet Union, and Germany. Nick sang "I'm Getting Nothing for Christmas." Holidays around the world—I didn't realize then that this theme predicted so well Nick's global journey as a superstar.

Nick thrived onstage. I discovered that he was unstoppable once he had an audience encouraging him with their applause!

Nick and the Singing Ex-Nun

One of the most unusual, talented, hardworking, and savvy of Nick's mentors was a woman named

Yvonne Cummings. As a young girl she joined the convent. Her desire to have children of her own derailed her religious calling. She left the convent to have a family and eventually raised two sons. Those child-rearing experiences with her two boys inspired her to write a television script. Yvonne put my son on television in an award-winning program.

She selected Nick out of an auditioning pack of children when she heard him sing, casting him as the leader of the pack of kids in the show she wrote and produced called *The Clubhouse Kids*. Her son's antics became Nick's scripts. The way she described it to the parents was that it was a bit like the classic *Little Rascals* with real moral values underneath the songs and the skits.

Yvonne showed me all her credentials, which she carried with her pasted impressively in a scrapbook. I thought to myself, Here is a woman with previous work as a real director, with a resume, and with the instinct to *hire* my son. I may have been correct about Yvonne's experience, but I was not correct about the word *hire*.

Nick would be starring in a television show to be aired on our local Florida cable channel, but he wouldn't be paid. In fact, all of us parents were asked to chip in with the expenses. Yvonne, it turned out, was a single mom and an aspiring creative producer without the financial backing she needed to develop and actually produce this program. She was sure that if we mothers and fathers just financed the pilot, then eventually the program would find a place on a major television network.

So I paid my forty dollars a month along with the

others and took Nick to rehearsals one day a week in church basements. Nick enjoyed the work and was getting lots of good experience. I'll never forget the taping of Yvonne's pilot. I drove Nick to the location. It was way out in the country. We parked and started walking . . . and walking until we were out in a cow pasture. It was lights, camera, action, and don't step in the cow patties.

Yvonne was wonderful with the children and with Nick especially. Her Thanksgiving special, "Griswald the Turkey," featured Nick and others chasing down a real live turkey. We chipped in, of course, for the turkey, too, who gave a great performance outrunning the children to avoid becoming the holiday dinner.

The Clubhouse Kids program aired on cable and won the Golden Cassette award. It went on to be nominated for many other national video awards, but, alas, never found a home on ABC, CBS, or NBC.

Nick did profit professionally, though, getting another commodity from this opportunity—news coverage. This marked the first moment that Nick had reporters asking him questions, reviewing his work, even quoting him. All the Tampa newspapers ran stories about the show. The *Tampa Times* headline on June 23, 1990, read: "TV's *Clubhouse Kids* Channels Children's Energy."

When the reporter asked Nick for a reaction to his role, he replied, "I like it. It's the funnest thing I can do." Not very articulate I agree, but Nick did get across his absolute love of what he was doing.

I can't move on, though, without sharing a few

more of the writer's comments and Yvonne's, which give new meaning to the warning "don't believe everything you read."

The writer said, "Promotion doesn't equal stardom for these [*Clubhouse Kids*] children. The search for the next River Phoenix or the New Kids on the Block is not taking place here." Obviously they underestimated Nick's star quality. Then Yvonne adds, "The parents that want agents steer clear of me because they know I'm not out to make their child a superstar."

Well, Yvonne wasn't out to make Nick a superstar, but she did nurture his talent and give him lots of practice. She failed to consider the fates or Nick's vision, which had superstar written all over it.

Don't You Step on My Blue Suede Shoes, White Leather Boots, or Black Velvet Cuffs

---

The Clubhouse Kids episodes turned out to be the best education in show business Nick and I had had. During the rehearsals, parents were welcome to watch. I met other parents. And I found myself on the receiving end of more advice, which I followed. I signed Nick up at a few talent agencies and took him for "head shots," which cost more money.

During this period Nick won the favor of two women who proved great for his career. The first was a woman, a no-nonsense vocal coach named Marianne Prinkey. It was a local agent who introduced me

The young dreamboat

Nick on his way up . . . and at the top.

n
I
c
K

N
i
C
K

to Marianne. Ms. Prinkey had "good connections" in the music world, I was assured, and had worked with the likes of Whitney Houston and other famous artists.

Marianne would consider working with Nick, but only after he auditioned for her for a fee of twenty-five dollars. At the time that seemed like a small price to pay so that Nick could have access to a woman who knew all the right people and was in the thick of the entertainment business. Nick impressed Marianne with his performance, as well as another woman whom we met, a well-known dance instructor, choreographer, and entrepreneur—Sandy Karl. Sandy owned The Karl and DiMarco School of Theater in Tampa. Once Nick teamed up with Marianne Prinkey and Sandy Karl, his skills became more polished and his showbiz experiences reached larger audiences and greater heights.

The first time she met Nick, Marianne showed me how to help him sing from his diaphragm. Under her weekly vocal instruction I started to see a lot of improvement in Nick's sound. Even more startling was the confidence I saw building. Marianne put together Talent Showcases featuring Nick and her other students. Although they were designed primarily to promote her talent agency, these recitals thrust Nick in front of large audiences.

Nick was thrilled to work with Marianne. She seemed to know how to get the best performance out of Nick every time. He loved singing the oldies. The audiences were crazy about Nick, a powerhouse performer in their eyes for such a youngster. Some of his more popular numbers included "Jailhouse Rock" and "Whole Lotta Shakin' Goin' On." Before long Nick built up a repertoire that included more than forty songs, which are included on the following pages.

Nick's voice became so powerful that Marianne had to teach him how to pull the microphone back during certain moments of the song. Good thing Nick had that vocal strength, because talent showcases weren't always perfect. I remember once all the microphones died. Nick, in the best tradition of "the show must go on," just kept singing and the audience still heard his every word.

What Marianne did for Nick's vocals, Sandy did for his dancing moves. Sandy ran a dance studio and also did all the choreography for the Swashbucklers, the Tampa Bay Buccaneers Cheerleading Squad. I have to say that without her Nick may never have become the star he is today. Sandy went out of her way many times for him. She had a knack for working with singers, and she choreographed whole numbers around Nick. Cheerleaders and her dancing school students swirled and toe-tapped behind Nick as he belted out his number, "Hound Dog," one year. The following season, "Rockin' Around the Christmas Tree" rocked the stadium. As a featured part of the Tampa Bay Buccaneers halftime extravaganzas, Nick's audience swelled to crowds of 55,000 or more football fans.

Nick felt right at home in amphitheaters from the

The Nick Carter Song List

1. "Chicago"
2. "Wind Beneath My Wings"
3. "Great Balls of Fire"
4. "Whole Lotta Shakin' Goin' On"
5. "Surfer Girl"
6. "Be True to Your School"
7. "Wouldn't It Be Nice"
8. "Easy Lover"
9. "You Can't Hurry Love"
10. "Rocket Man"
11. "Candle in the Wind"
12. "Your Song"
13. "Bennie and the Jets"
14. "Saturday Night's Alright for Fighting"
15. "Twist and Shout"
16. "Dark Horse"
17. "This Song"
18. "Got My Mind Set on You"
19. "God Bless the U. S. A."
20. "Sunshine on My Shoulders"
21. "Annie's Song"
22. "Thank God I'm a Country Boy"
23. "All I Ask of You"
24. "Shall We Dance"
25. "Only the Lonely"
26. "Pretty Woman"
27. "Johnny B. Goode"
28. "Sweet Little Sixteen"
29. "Stand by Me"
30. "Hound Dog"
31. "My Way"
32. "Jailhouse Rock"
33. "Tell Her About It"
34. "Uptown Girl"
35. "Don't Be Cruel"
36. "All Shook Up"
37. "Blue Suede Shoes"
38. "It's Still Rock and Roll to Me"
39. "Let's Hang On!"
40. "Anything You Can Do I Can Do Better"
41. "California Girls"

Nick's Christmas and Holiday Songs

1. "Jingle Bell Rock"
2. "Blue Christmas"
3. "Rockin' Around the Christmas Tree"
4. "Feliz Navidad"
5. "Merry Christmas Darling"
6. "Please Come Home for Christmas"

start. It's no surprise that when I see him on a gigantic stadium stage now, he's so comfortable. A stage, the bigger the better, and a spotlight, the brighter the better, are Nick's milk and honey.

During the Sandy and Marianne years, Nick participated in many national dance competitions, local and regional. Dance and singing competitions brought out his best. He participated in some of the biggest and the most intense song and dance category rivalries in our area. One that stands out in my mind is his performance of "Love Is a Wonderful Thing." He blew away the rest of the contestants, who stood around with worried expressions as he performed.

Nick wore many costumes during this time. He wore each one, even a few doosies, with unabashed pride! Just as I once created his Halloween costumes, now my sewing machine worked overtime to invent outfits for many of these performances.

For one show, Nick suited up in a gold lamé astronaut costume I created. Its flaming yellow color set off his blond hair. It had a big wide belt. Nick wore white leather boots. He looked the part of a space-age rocket man as he sang Elton John's classic hit song.

At a Showstoppers National Dance Competition in Myrtle Beach, South Carolina, Nick, dressed like a miniature Elvis in Las Vegas splendor, took home the trophy. Nick swiveled, decked out to the nines in a sparkling bright white suit that I had fashioned with a multicolored sprinkling of gemstones. White fringe ran up the seams of Nick's pants, from his ankles all the way up to his waist. Nick pulled off a lively Elvis impersonation, perfecting that Presley pout, and making the girls giggle and swoon just like that Memphis man. (Actually I think I'm going to get this Elvis costume out and try it on Aaron.)

I cannot forget the MC Hammer performance. In black velvet Hammer pants, a cross between bell-bottoms and droopy drawers, Nick rapped "You Can't Touch This." Nick bounced across the stage in hip-hop choreography, rapping as articulately, I think, as Hammer himself. Everyone clapped and stomped to the rhythm while bursts of applause and praise erupted several times. No one else could touch him that day.

Perhaps the most famous competition that Nick won was the New Original Amateur Hour that took place at Universal Studios in Orlando, with Willard Scott as the master of ceremonies. When Nick sang, the crowd just went wild. I overheard many people saying things like, "Who is this kid?" "Do you believe the seasoned performance coming out of the mouth of such a youngster?" "What personality!" Nick felt like a true star that day.

During those years Nick performed anywhere, anytime, for anyone willing to listen. Even with Marianne and Sandy booking Nick, he craved more. A Nick show headlined every Carter family gathering. When Bob and I had friends over to our house for a barbecue, Nick hauled the karaoke machine from the garage. He set it up poolside. Any children who came as guests, Nick recruited for the stage show, casting them as his backup band or chorus line. He would turn out the lights, except for a makeshift spotlight, put on the music, and give a razzle-dazzle live performance.

Nick warmed up with these impromptu shows. Performing in front of a captive audience of relatives and friends was good practice for a future that waited for him just over the horizon.

Ticket to the Future

As part of our triple threat strategy of letting Nick sing, dance, and act, he pursued an assortment of acting opportunities in Florida. He landed parts in commercials for The Money Store and The Florida State Lottery. In a public service spot produced by a European clothing line, Nick poignantly acted the part of an emotionally bruised boy, victimized by a verbally abusive father. His role, and even the entire spot was brief, but so moving. Nick's acting ability began to show.

A Florida bus company decided to make a film titled *Ticket to the Future.* Nick played the leading character, who instructed the audience on how to use the bus system. (Okay, so it was a long way from Keanu Reeves in *Speed.*) The story line journeyed from the present day into the future. Then the bus transformed into a futuristic space shuttle. Once again, Nick played a kind of rocket man.

A local Florida public library produced an instructional film in which Nick had the main part. He memorized a very long script, lots of lines, songs, and dance steps. The movie aimed to teach children the basics of how to use the library. Nick knows more about researching in the library than his fans would ever guess!

There may be stars in the recording and film industry who blasted overnight to success. Or others who got lucky and awakened in a full-blown storm of fame and fortune. My son was not one of them. Although it seems as if Nick has catapulted to superstardom at a high-flying speed, that is an illusion. Nick Carter did not jump out of the pages of a Hollywood potboiler. Slowly but surely, in jerks and starts, he made progress. Each little bit part and three-minute songfest added more luster to his aura, more fuel to the velocity of his star-bound trajectory. He made it to the top in show business one dance step, one song, one page at a time. Mentors Rick D'Onofrio, Yvonne Cummings, Marianne Prinkey, and Sandy Karl played invaluable parts in this great accomplishment.

Nick spent his young adolescent years from the age of ten onward working extremely hard at developing his talent. He practiced and practiced vocal exercises. He watched his image in the dance studio mirror for endless hours, synchronizing his rhythm and refining the technique. He read and spoke lines this way and that way, struggling to find the right emotional chord. I watched him, and helped him, hone all of his singing, dancing, and acting skills.

The people in Nick's early professional years truly acted like angels, watching over my son and nourishing his creative spirit. At other times, Nick battled in a back-stabbing, cutthroat theatrical netherworld. Simultaneously, he faced ridicule and rivalry and fought back with fanatical focus and devotion to his crafts. Nick never let anyone or anything stand in his way. He saw beyond the moment to a future he never lost sight of.

Many other talented singers, dancers, musicians, and actors, both boys and girls, always surrounded Nick. What made his star shine brighter? What accounted for his rising above a pack of extremely talented and gifted contemporaries?

Now I know that I am prejudiced where Nick Carter is concerned. Still, I sincerely believe there are concrete reasons why Nick has risen to stardom and left others in his trail of stardust. The mentors in Nick's life laid out advice and guidance, and he took advantage of every guiding strategy. Here's exactly how he proceeded:

- *Nick soaked up know-how like a little sponge.* I watched Nick in a variety of stage productions starting with St. Petersburg's *Peter and the Wolf,* and *Holidays Around the World.* He observed. Nick carefully watched every move the seasoned actors and professional singers made. He picked up tidbits of knowledge and insiders' secrets.

- *Nick listened to instructions.* The first time that Marianne gave Nick a tip on improving his phrasing of a song, or his posture, he listened with rapt attention. When she pointed to her diaphragm during a lesson, Nick touched his to get it working. He followed every creative order.

- *Nick accepted and learned from criticism.* As a youngster, when Nick was criticized for his dancing deficits, he didn't complain or lash out. Rather than whine or balk, he put his heels to the grindstone.

- *Nick did his homework.* I'm not talking about his arithmetic problems or memorizing his vocabulary words, although he did that kind of homework, too. Nick learned the lines in a play, the words to a song, the scene in a script, or the dance steps in a routine. Or a combination of any or all of those. Showbiz comes with homework. Nick always aimed for an A.

- *Nick acted responsibly.* I know Nick has a reputation for being a cutup, a joker. I am not going to tell you that he isn't playful, even a bit wild at times. I will tell you when it came to taking his dance routine, his musical number, or a scene in a script or a commercial seriously, Nick always demonstrated a mature outlook. He didn't waste anyone's time. He came prepared, ready to perform. He did what he set out to do.

- *Nick stayed focused.* Of all Nick's character traits this is, perhaps, the one most responsible for his stardom. Nick kept his goals in his sights no matter what. He started young in a sophisticated entertainment business world. He had pressures and distractions like any other preadolescent. He had crushes and anxieties. He carried the weight of expectations. He shouldered the sting of rejections. No one and nothing derailed Nick.

I was there with him, every beat and heartbeat of the way. We talked about everything. Nick gave it all he had to give. The spotlight highlights a finely tuned star. His performance is even more, though. Nick sings with all of his body and soul . . . from the heart.

10

Must Every Cinderella Tale Have a Wicked Stage Mother?

No one talks about my son Nick's success without suggesting it all reads like a fairy tale. I think his rise to superstardom is more like a Horatio Alger tale, because his really is a self-made success. Nick was no ragamuffin Cinderella, transformed into rock royalty by a fairy godmother. He started out with very little in the way of material things . . . and with music in his soul. He had the willingness to do whatever was necessary to make that music louder, clearer, and better. It took about four years of trying, knocking on doors, and getting rejected, before Nick's dreams came true. His story was no twist of fate.

As much as anything, the Nick Carter story is a family story, one of mothers and fathers and children, and hopes and dreams. I've been criticized over the years, sometimes severely by many people. Let's face it, every fairy tale has to have a wicked character.

Cinderella had her mean stepmother, overworking her. Snow White had the mean queen, overworking her and attempting murder with poison. And so it didn't surprise me when I got branded early on in Nick Carter's fairy tale as the evil mother.

I've been stereotyped as the most deadly of ogres: stage mother. This monster is ruthless. She'll do anything, step over anyone, stab even her best friend in the back in order to get her way. She is ambitious. The stage mother's ambition is not the good kind, either. It's downright unhealthy. Her drive is seen as obsessive, overshadowing what's good for her child. She is that kind of subtle intimidator who gets her child to do her bidding, as if the poor youngster was nothing more than a slave—a miserable, browbeaten little slave.

The stepmother's motives are suspect. She is deviously bent on furthering her own frustrated, starstruck aspirations at any costs. She's after wealth, absolute power, and she's stupid because she rejects everyone's advice on developing the career of her child.

The stage mother is almost always drawn in caricature as this evil queen of the show business empire. I believe, too, that in most cases it's a myth, a colorful myth, but a myth nonetheless. It survives and is almost universal, I think, because it provides such sensational fodder for stories about young stars, selling tabloids, newspapers, magazines, even movies. I had to battle this image with Nick. Now with Aaron, I am battling it all over again.

While Aaron and I were in Germany last winter, one of the newspapers featured a classic stage mother smear story, accompanied by a photograph of Aaron and myself. The snooping photographer stalked us until the end of a long day in a foreign country as we battled jet lag and the frustration of trying to get to our appointments in a strange land. In the photograph Aaron isn't smiling and looks tired; I'm alongside. The caption translates: "Poor unhappy child star pushed to the brink of exhaustion by his pushy and uncaring stage mother." How unfair!

It is regrettable that the parent of a child star automatically becomes a target. There are people in the industry who would like nothing better than for the parent or guardian of an underage performer to get lost. They want free rein over the child's entire life. I refused to buckle. I would not turn over my parental responsibility for Nick. I will not do so with Aaron.

Whose Dream of Stardom Is It Anyway?

The mother of a child star is pigeonholed as some kind of driving tyrant because of this question: How could a youngster of five or six, or eight or nine even, know that he wants to be in show business? Well, I can say emphatically that Nick knew what he wanted. He wanted to sing and star in a show. He sang in the backyard. He created stage shows on the family trampoline. He imagined his audience in the blades of grass. He looked for applause in the attentions of the Peeping Tom neighboring kids who looked through the fence and egged Nick on for trampoline encores. This was Nick's doing, not mine. I didn't pin any starcrazed dreams that were mine on my son.

Yes, I did run and get Bob and rummage through the Yellow Pages with excitement looking for a vocal teacher. Yes, I was the one who bought the newspapers and carefully looked through the entertainment sections for news of auditions.

Was I the one who went shopping with Nick and picked out the clothes that would show him off in the best light? Did I take him for hair cuts and to photo sessions? Did I sew costumes? Did I sit at the typewriter and write out a resume? Yes, yes, I plead guilty to all this and more.

I did this for Nick, not for myself. I know my own motives. I knew my son and he knows me. Nick couldn't do what he wanted to do, or get to where he wanted to go without my help because he was a child. Adults with a goal can get in the car, or get on the phone and put a plan into action. A child can't. A child cannot achieve a dream without the support, the guidance, and the encouragement of an adult. I became a significant influence in his life and in his early career because I was a mother who wanted to see her son happy and fulfilled.

I was very fortunate to be able to work at home and develop a close bond with Nick. When I saw his musical abilities I thought of the Biblical parable about not hiding one's light under a bushel. I made the calls and the appointments. I was the wheels. I helped Nick find a bigger spotlight than the one he constructed with living room lamps in front of our family video camera.

Some children are drawn to playing ball. Their

parents buy them a bat and a baseball and then sign them up for Little League. Nick was drawn to the entertainment field and so I signed him up for the vocal and dance coaches rather than the athletic ones.

It was Nick who insisted on going to the auditions and shows, not me. We both enjoyed it. The real test is the nag test. Did I ever have to nudge Nick to perform? Did I ever have to nag him to work on that song for June Daniels, "Go Fly a Kite"? Did I ever have to remind him that Tuesday night was *The Clubhouse Kids'* rehearsal and he had to learn his lines? Never. I never had to nag Nick because he just loved doing anything that revolved around music or performing.

That is the key to becoming successful in the entertainment industry for a person of any age. Going into show business is not something that one person can decide for another. A parent can encourage. A parent must support and be prepared to sacrifice both time and money to help a child achieve a goal. A parent does have to do some of the work involved, but if the goal and commitment aren't first and foremost in the heart and soul of the child the whole enterprise is doomed.

The Showbiz Bug Bit Nick Badly

Nick was a competitive child. He had no choice. He grew up in a large family where his brother and sisters competed with him for my time. Then there were all the elderly extended grandparents, aunts, and uncles who also wanted some of his mom's attention. Nick learned how to win attention. He developed a healthy competitive nature. He took that attitude into the world of show business.

Auditions resembled competitive sports for Nick. Just like in a ball game, there are winners and losers. A player has to practice skills, and psych himself up just before game time. The crowd is always watching, ready to boo or applaud. The thrill of victory feels good. Nick was always game for another whack at the competition. If there was an audition, he wanted to go for it.

After Nick finished his run in *Peter and the Wolf,* I was dog tired. Even Nick's baby blues looked a little bleary. We had to drive all the way up to St. Petersburg twice a week for rehearsals. Once the play opened, it ran in Tampa and then the cast took it on the road to schools in the area. It was an extremely hectic time, getting Nick to this performance and that. I had to rearrange lessons, talk to Nick's teachers about letting him leave school early, and plan ahead to make sure my obligations were met on the home front. As the end of the run drew near, I couldn't even imagine considering another audition for a long time.

Hard as it is to believe, even while Nick gave *Peter and the Wolf* all he had to give, he contemplated a new opportunity. The *Tampa Tribune* ran an announcement that auditions would be held for children between the ages of six and twelve for an upcoming television program to be filmed in our area.

I hesitated for an instant, but immediately showed the notice to Nick. Before I could even get out the words, "Do you want to try out for it, Nick?" my son glanced at me and said, "Mom, a real television part. . . . Can I try out for it?"

I did add, "Are you sure you want to do this, Nick? Don't you want to take a breather after this play?"

"No! I really want to try and do this." The look in Nick's eyes and the urgency in his voice told me that he was already imagining landing his first part on TV. Nick had the bug. He couldn't resist going to yet another audition, just to see. . . .

Nick loved testing himself with each audition. Could he measure up to the expectations of the producer, director, agent, or vocal coach? Could he blow the competition out of the water? Would he win the part? This trial by fire, the fight to the finish, essentially became mine, too, by association.

Nick had the determination of an adult. He may have been a child, but his willpower and drive was that of one much older. I treated Nick the singer like an adult. I respected what he wanted. Because Nick the child was powerless, as the adult in his life I empowered him to make that next audition, to take that next step, to arrive at that next opening night.

Someone to Watch over Nick . . . And Now Aaron

The music business in particular, and the entertainment world in general, are populated by some people who have their own special agendas that may place the welfare of a child star at the bottom.

Nick and I met many wonderful and caring individuals during the early years of his career. However, we also found ourselves in situations with people who didn't pay much attention to his feelings. Over the years I challenged those who wanted to play puppeteer and jerk Nick's strings without considering his well-being. A child, no matter how talented, is vulnerable. Nick at nine or thirteen was not old enough to confront adults about his rights. I would have been less than conscientious if I did not stand up for Nick and protect him against those who saw him as a product, or a photograph, or as a performance. This applied whether we were at an audition, a rehearsal, or a shoot.

When Nick was a child I attempted to bring him to full flower both as an entertainer and as an authentic human being. I took my responsibility as Nick's mother, his protector, and his nurturer seriously. I've always considered it part of my job to insist that Nick be treated cordially and with respect. My insistence hasn't always been in sync with everyone else's. I've been an immovable force on this issue.

The protocol for mothers at the auditions in Tampa was for them to make themselves scarce. Because Nick was only ten or eleven, I insisted on being with him at all times, except when he actually went into the room to read for a part.

I sensed that Nick appreciated my being nearby.

He always made eye contact with me and I know my reassurance affected his performance. I knew with me in the wings, busy professional photographers, talent agents, scouts, or whoever would think twice before dismissing my child rudely or impatiently.

Nick felt happier when I was on hand when the curtain went up. When the curtain "crashed" he needed me even more urgently.

Nick had some heady experiences for a preteen. He was on the set for the making of *Edward Scissorhands.* We traveled to Burt Reynolds's ranch near Miami where filming of *Cop and a Half* took place. On both of these movie sets Nick encountered disappointments. Nick got the part in *Edward Scissorhands,* but its star, Johnny Depp, didn't acknowledge Nick at all. Our trip to the Reynolds set didn't have the happy ending of Nick getting the part for which he read. For a young boy like Nick with stars in his eyes, not getting picked, and not getting taken aside for a few words of encouragement, was very hard to take.

It was my job, and a very important one, to make sure that Nick felt okay when things didn't go as we planned. I always reassured Nick with words like, "It's not you, Nick. They were looking for another type, a different look, a certain personality. The producer had another idea in mind." Or I'd say, "Nick, you did a fine job, but it wasn't meant to be."

Nick had many successful coups, but he also had countless letdowns. Waiting for callbacks was a sit-on-the-edge-of-your-seat drama and early on Nick suffered through a host of rejections.

I'd always tell Nick not to worry. I always played down the winning versus losing angle because I knew that Nick often thought in these terms. I emphasized that this goal of performing wasn't everything, or the only important thing in life. I recast Nick's failures, insisting he look at them as just another step in an attempt to get his foot in the door. If the callback never came, or when another boy got the part, I'd tell Nick to just forget about it. I'd say, "Go ride your bike" or "Go play Nintendo or ball with Aaron." Nick was a child-star-in-the-making, but I wanted him to always remember he was a child first, a star-in-the-making on the side.

I made certain that Nick had the time to be a child. Whether Nick worked on a modeling shoot or on an industrial film, whether he was onstage in a rehearsal or in front of rolling television cameras, I kept to the schedule without losing sight of what was fair and healthy for Nick.

It has always been my sacred duty to make sure that Nick maintains a sense of well-being, a sense of honor, a sense of family, and a love of life. I never want him to feel that he is out in the world all alone, twisting in the fickle winds of popularity, alone in the crowd, as they say. I never want Nick to experience that. My job is to make sure that a sense of isolation, loneliness at the top, doesn't define Nick . . . or Aaron.

Bob and I juggled—and still juggle—our lives to be there for Nick as much as we can and still be available, loving parents to our other children. In spite of what at times seemed like insurmountable obstacles over the years, I have stood firm. I am a dedicated mother, and what I think a good mother should be. So when people glance at me sideways and mutter "stage mother," I live with it.

As I watched Nick's success rise above the bounds of his dreams, and as I watch Aaron hip hop in Nick's footsteps, I have become an avid reader and a celebrity watcher. I pay close attention to any series about child stars and teen idols, like the recent VH1 program about the rise and fall of Andy Gibb, the youngest brother of the BeeGees. I read biographies and autobiographies like *Moonwalk,* in which Michael Jackson tells his child-star story, the good, the bad, and the ugly parts. The lesson that the entertainment business is very hard on children and adolescents has not escaped me, or Nick.

I tried to make sure from the start that Nick wasn't hurt or demoralized. I believe that a strong family and keeping in close touch is the way that Nick and Aaron can embrace success and still thrive personally.

The Nick Carter story is no fairy tale. He's not going to go *poof* after midnight. I never was a wicked stepmother-type stage mother. Still, though there's no fairy tale involved, I do hope with all my heart that all the Carters live happily ever after.

11

☆ On a Grinding Tour ☆

Success for the Backstreet Boys didn't happen because Nick and the guys lounged around humming "Quit Playing Games with My Heart" and trying on Tommy Hilfiger clothes.

Life spent working, rehearsing, performing was often a grind. And I'm not talking about *The Grind*, the MTV special. Someone taped that performance for me. In *Spring Break in the Bahamas*, Nick wore a silly-looking fishing hat to protect himself from the sun and a tropical-print shirt that billowed in the Caribbean breezes. I loved the show, but for an instant while I watched it, I felt melancholy, wishing that in truth Nick was just another carefree teenager on vacation.

Nick frequently sings "Let's Have a Party." Sometimes the song blares from a tropical paradise setting. Or it Americanizes a foreign stage. The fans in the audience *are* having a party. You can see it in their excited faces, in their swaying bodies. Nick looks like one of them, but he isn't. He is at the party, but he's working.

I've looked at his grueling schedule many times and asked him if he's really happy. He always reassures me, saying something like, "Yes, Mom, absolutely!"

The lifestyle of a pop star is not always what a fan might think it is. There are those few glorious hours up on stage. Then there are the hours and hours Nick spends looking out of windows. It might be at an airport terminal where Nick's watching airplanes land and take off while he waits for his flight, biting his nails. (The reports are true. He doesn't like flying.) Or he's looking out over the wing of a 747 into the clouds. Whether Nick is on a plane, in the tour bus, or even a stretch limousine, it's always the same.

Nick is on the inside of fame looking out . . . while he works. On the Hollywood stage at the MTV awards he's rubbing elbows with the rock'n'roll "in crowd," flirting with the likes of Monica, Mariah, and Madonna, and trading on-the-road war stories with Boyz II Men or another group. In a photo shoot for *Teen People* magazine Nick's in a swanky Beverly Hills hotel pool. My, oh my, it sure does look like a charmed and glamorous life, doesn't it?

The reality beneath the shine and the sheen of the star machinery has a hard edge. Wherever there are celebrities, there are egos; artists compete for attention and jockey for position. Life in the spotlight is a business where there's more working going on than socializing.

Every time you catch Nick swiveling his hips in a dance routine, you can be sure hours and hours of rehearsal preceded it. Panache and practice are inseparable. The music video you watch only lasts a few minutes. The production work and rehearsals stretch from dawn until dusk. Then the finished product has to be filmed fast, in a day or two. The pressure is intense.

It wasn't a snap for Nick to learn the Spanish lyrics for "I'll Never Break Your Heart." He had to learn proper pronunciation, memorize the lyrics, and sound as if he's been speaking Spanish all his life. Then he had to lip-synch it precisely. Aaron got a lesson in the cold reality of show business when he filmed his music video for "Surfin USA." He was on the beach in Santa Monica and the surf did tickle his ankles . . . but those ankles turned blue. It was freezing and cloudy. Aaron had to pretend it was the perfect California sun and fun day.

When fans go to concerts, they have a ball. The adrenaline rushes through every girl anticipating the moment when the curtain goes up and Nick appears in flesh and blood. Electricity bolts and buzzes from fan to fan as Nick sings. When Nick smiles, the girls explode with screeching laughter and the bliss of young love. Going to a concert, watching Nick show his stuff, is sheer fun. I've seen it from the wings.

For Nick there's nothing glamorous about the tight schedule and the repetition. Town after town. Venue after venue. Cheeseburger after cheeseburger. Hotel room after hotel room. The roar of the crowd washes over Nick and fills him with joy, but it also drains him. Mister "Am I Sexual" flops into another hotel bed simply Mister "Am I Exhausted"—or Mister "Am I Hungry" . . . with nary a Swiss roll or pint of milk in sight.

Nick sits patiently for hours giving interviews to journalists when he'd rather be spending that time talking on the cell phone to his friends. He dresses and undresses in a succession of outfits for photo shoots, when what he'd really like to be doing is walking in and out of stores at the mall. Nick does, and always has done, what is required to make his dream come true: work hard.

When Nick comes home, he runs around almost frantically trying to squeeze in a social life. His touring commitments leave only a few days off here and there. He crams in hours on the beach with afternoons over at Disney. Don't forget, Nick is a teenager. After such a marathon funfest I frequently see the light on in Nick's bedroom and climb the stairs only to find my superstar has crashed, sleeping in his clothes, too tired to change or even flip off the light.

Nick gives one hundred percent of himself, trying to play hard without skimping on the work that is expected of him as a superstar. My boy started working like a man at thirteen. At moments when I look down at Nick sleeping, perhaps with sand still between the toes that are sticking out from under the sheets, I'm very thankful that he is young and healthy. But I worry that in some ways he is too mature, too responsible for an eighteen-year-old.

Teenagers are trying to find out who they are. They look for answers to such questions as "Am I lovable?" and "Am I sexual?" They try to find their place out in the world, alone, away from parents. My son tries to find his answers just like any other teenage guy, except that his fame complicates the questions. He wonders if people like him for himself or for his celebrity, if girls see the real Nick, the normal one, or some unreal image? Nick, like all his peers, has to find answers for himself. It's not simple when you work so much and are always in the limelight.

A parade of songwriters send him songs. A pack of screenwriters send him scripts. Fans send him reams of appreciation. Venue promoters want to book an endless calendar of stage shows. Nick's future looks bright, but full of more hard work.

Does he get sidetracked by the glitz of fame or distracted by all the offers coming in? I don't think so. He may be a superstar, but he never forgets that he wants to give each and every fan his best performance, body and soul. Nick's fans mean everything to him because it is their love and loyalty that fueled his rocketship to stardom.

Nick and I talked about his future one afternoon in a rare quiet moment for us at home in Florida, as we dangled our toes over the dock out back. I asked what direction he wanted to take.

"My number one love is my music," he said. "I've done acting, but I thought at the time that I wasn't that good at it." Nick looked over at me for . . . what? Approval? Argument? "Maybe I can be good. I think," Nick says, "that I'll stick to music for now. I see people like me get so many opportunities and they take them all. They get into too many things and lose track of what they originally did so well. I'm willing to try new things, like the cameo for Aaron's new television pilot. I'll never say never because you don't know what the future holds, Mom. I live every day, day by day, just doing my best."

I'm sure Nick's fans will be glad to hear those words. I certainly was. Nick convinced me that he not only knows the value of hard work, but he knows how to value his work.

Caring, Kindness . . . and Getting Bashed

A recent article contained a paragraph that described my son brushing off a fan in a wheelchair. I saw red. Of course, Nick didn't know what this writer was talking about! I knew it was ridiculous! Nick would never turn his back on someone with a disability in that callous way. He couldn't treat a person in a wheelchair unkindly, because that kind of cruel insensitivity simply isn't a part of his character.

Part of me wanted to track down that writer and disprove the charge, but Nick and I agree that such negative portrayals have to be chalked up to the downside of being famous. Once on top, you're fair game for a breed of media opportunists who want to write negative, critical stories. You have to just shrug it off.

Clearly, the writer of that anecdote didn't know

that taking care of the elderly and the infirm was the Carter family business. She didn't know that as a toddler Nick lived in The Pleasant View Retirement Home in Westfield, New York. From the age of four, he grew up in and then among our residents in our Tampa residential home, The Garden Villa, A Home for the Elderly.

Our elder-care facility was a family enterprise that gave a larger extended family first to Nick and BJ, then to the three other children as they came along. Nick lived among the ailing elderly, as well as those with a range of disabilities. Over the years, our extended family included a blind man and victims of cancer, Parkinson's disease, emphysema, and multiple sclerosis. We cared for paraplegics who went through life in wheelchairs, and patients suffering from dementia, other mental illnesses, and Alzheimer's.

Our family didn't live separate from our patients. Our bedrooms were near one another. We ate dinner together. Life then was at times a bit like *One Flew Over the Cuckoo's Nest* and *The Waltons*. I'd hear a patient say "Good night, Nick." Then little Nicky answered, "Good night, Robert." "Good night, BJ," echoed down the hall, followed by, "Good night, Helen."

These folks, some in their twilight years and others with physical and mental burdens, had a profound effect on Nick.

Wheeling Through the A B Cs

Helen, our very first boarder, who was primarily responsible for our moving our retirement home business to Florida, had been a kindergarten teacher. Never married, she treated Nick and BJ as if they were her own grandchildren. In every sense of the word, they were.

I was a working mom. I had lots of people to take care of every day. There were meals to cook, and bedsheets to wash and hang out to dry. Our patients needed emotional care. Taking time to listen to a story demanded equal time with chores. Helen often watched over Nick and BJ.

It was in Helen's lap that Nick learned his ABCs. Many afternoons, I'd pass by her bedroom or the living room and there she'd be with Nick, the two turning the pages of a Golden Book. Helen would read the words slowly to the delight of Nick, who'd look at the pages with rapt attention. She would sing and Nick would try to keep up with the lyrics that lilted through the windows, surfing on the breeze, and on upstairs where I'd be working. It was Helen who praised Nick when he drew that perfect letter with a brown crayon. She complimented Nick on his first artwork and Crayola valentines that we hung on our refrigerator. How often I worked to the sound of Helen singing nursery rhymes to Nick.

When Christmastime came around Helen acted just like a child again. Her favorite thing was seeing all the holiday lights decorating the outside of houses. So we'd roll her wheelchair out to the family car, Nick would pile in, and I'd get behind the wheel. Off we'd go, sharing the spirit of youngsters, in search of the best decorated and illuminated homes. We brought this ritual to Florida, too. Perhaps all transplanted Northerners need to search out the sights of Christmas, whether there are pines or palm trees standing next to Santa Claus and his reindeer.

When we lived in Tampa, Nick would often come home from school and wheel Helen outside. My children frequently played under her watchful and loving eye. She kept them out of mischief and reminded them to mind their p's and q's. At dinnertime, she urged them to eat their peas.

BJ and Nick still talk about the battles over green peas! Nick, BJ, and I sat around the kitchen table a few months ago, and BJ remembered, "I never liked peas, but Helen insisted I eat them. Now I'm grown and I love peas!" With that Nick and BJ toasted each other with a big forkful of—green peas.

Nick learned so much from Helen. Not only those early ABCs or beginning to sound out words, he came to understand, innocently and wordlessly, that the wisdom and warmth he felt sitting on Helen's lap had nothing to do with the fact that a wheelchair bolstered it. He knew even as a child that love and caring lived within many less-than-perfect bodies.

Nick saw that all people had more in common than not. Feeling awe at the glimmer of Christmas lights, savoring the guilty pleasure of a stolen cookie, all human beings shared the same appetites and desires, regardless of the shape of their body or the strength of their limbs. No one had to instruct my Nick, or my other children, in the rights or the dignity of the disabled or handicapped. My kids were way ahead of the rest of the population in the lessons of diversity. Nick actually could instruct the larger world on this issue.

Nick learned how to nurture while he was being nurtured by Helen and others. He became not only responsive, but attached. I shall never forget the sight of my son acting as a human crutch, helping one of our elderly residents walk across the room to a favorite chair. I saw his empathy. I felt his emotion. I shared—and was proud of—his compassion.

Playing with "Old Friends" After School

Nick and BJ and I talked the other day about our nursing home years.

BJ said to Nick, "Remember when I used to invite my friends home after school? Remember how they'd act when they saw the old people? They'd say, 'Euuu, how could you touch them!' I'd be hugging and kissing and telling our patients about my day. My friends just didn't understand."

Nick shook his head in agreement. "Remember Robert? And Fred?" This set Nick and BJ off into a hilarious imitation of the way each yelled for the other.

Nick recalled, "I have never forgotten Fred. I spent hours watching him carve little birds out of wood, whittling their wings and beaks. He gave me my first Swiss Army pocketknife and he showed me how to carve. He'd tell me stories all the while. A lot of the stories I can't remember, but I'll never forget the perfect birds."

Two boys with their red pocketknife sounds commonplace? Not really. Nick's apprenticeship to the elderly Fred went beyond that. Fred was an unusual wildlife sculptor. He often couldn't tell you the day of the week or who was the current president, but he knew exactly how long to carve the beak of a Baltimore oriole. Nick opened up to Fred, and others, realizing that each had a unique gift, and recognizing that even odd birds have something special to teach a boy who is wise enough to learn.

Each and every one of these elderly and fractured folks had stories to tell Nick. Although, as he says, he can't recall the details of any of those tales, they did profoundly contribute to his destiny. I, too, learned from my elderly class. The lesson that moved me most was one that governed the way I raised Nick and nurtured his dream.

Let me explain. When you care for older and sick men and women, you see firsthand that the opportunities and the dreams each one of them once had have slipped away. It is the nature of those who have reached old age to look back. Once someone gets to that time in life, they always look back with longing and sometimes also with regret. Some have more regret than others and point to the roads they should have taken, the people to whom they should have said "I'm sorry."

I spent a great deal of time along with Nick listening to folks talk about their life stories. I heard sad tales of fights between parents and children that ended in harsh words and hard feelings that were never undone. I saw the broken hearts and the unrequited love in the stories I was told as I sat on the side of a bed. Too many times I listened to "If only I had done this" or "I never should have done that."

Some of the patients that I took care of told Nick and me about jobs they spent their whole life working at, even though they hated their work. I saw that each and every one of them had a real story, a special talent, skill, or ability. Some of these men and women had been successful at fulfilling that special part of themselves. By doing so they were the happiest individuals. Others never achieved any of their dreams. Many times, the stories of their lives brought tears to my eyes because of the trials and tribulations they experienced, and because of the goals never realized.

I came away from those bedside confessional sessions with a clear conviction. It is a perspective that I have told Nick over and over again. When you are young, the future is wide open to you. Every old person's story underlined that simple truth. There is a world of opportunity right before the eyes of every young man and woman. If you see this, and seize the possibilities before you, you can go after what you want in life. The future belongs to you. It is within your grasp. It is out of your grasp only if you fail to try.

Every old soul who ever confessed a regret to Nick or to me should rest easier knowing that his or her mistakes or failures contributed to the success of my son. Nick and I listened on a daily basis to the hindsight of the older generation. I took that wisdom to heart. I savored it and saved it and repackaged it to teach to my children. The elderly who passed in and out of my life, and Nick's life, had an impact on his youth. The torch of possibility and hope literally passed from the dying into the soul of my children because I was determined to oversee that exchange.

Matters of Life and Death

Because these people were old and sometimes very sick, there was an extremely sad side to our extended family life. Nick got to know, and often became very attached to, people as they came to the end of their lives. These men and women radiated affection and caring toward my youngsters until their last breath. They shared the final shreds of emotion with my young boy who was open to these last gifts of friendship.

Nick and BJ came to know at an early age what human suffering is, what human agony entails, and even what death looks like. Yes, this was part and parcel of the Carter family. We pulled together to help each other, and to assist the older people who depended on us.

I'm sure there are some who think it was wrong of me to let my children see this side of life at such young ages. People have often said to me in no uncertain terms that they wouldn't want their son or daughter to witness, firsthand, so much illness and pain before the final pages in the lives of the suffering.

I feel differently. I always have. I knew that these events sensitized Nick. Here in Nick's own words is how he describes it. "Having the experience of knowing people and seeing them pass away, out of your life, made me sit back and actually mature. I experienced what a lot of people *didn't* at a young age. I matured to a greater extent than other kids because of it."

Nick naturally empathized with the anguish of the human condition. Having been exposed personally to the tragedies of the living, I knew my son would appreciate more profoundly the joys of life. Nick understood more urgently than many of his peers that each and every day is to be appreciated.

When you see human suffering, pathos, and even death, life takes on a very serious, very fragile, and very holy quality. You can't help but think of everything you encounter on a deeper level. That perspective is the legacy that our retirement home business left on Nick.

We are part of all the people with whom we have had the privilege and good fortune to come into contact—I truly believe that. Nick approaches people, young and old alike, with equal measures of worth and affection. I saw this first when he began performing in talent shows. The audiences back then in Tampa were not filled with ponytailed, screaming young teenagers. More often they were filled with large numbers of retirees and senior citizens. They responded to Nick with as much admiration as hordes of girls would later.

As a performer, Nick has always attracted people of all kinds and all ages. I suspect he carries with him some invisible tattoo from those early years. It may be hard to identify. Perhaps it's the way he looks right into someone's eyes and sees their spirit, not their age. Perhaps it's because his smile connects with the human spirit of joy that resides in any heart, young or old. Human beings mysteriously recognize and respond to someone who sees them as worthwhile and valuable. Many times I've seen my son reach out while performing and connect to every type of person applauding his song.

From the first Nick was blessed with good health and a large dose of beauty. He knows that not everyone is so fortunate. His life experience with our family health-care business, his extended family of live-in grandparents and offbeat aunts and uncles, gave him an appreciation of good health and of life, of the human spirit and of its value.

So when you read some nasty story that casts Nick Carter as insensitive, don't believe a word of it. Nick doesn't have an unkind bone in his body.

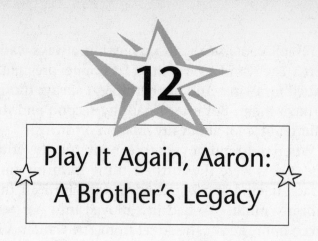

12

Play It Again, Aaron: A Brother's Legacy

Aaron was a surprise from the first minutes he stirred inside me.

The Birth of My Second-Generation Teen Idol

In both my family and my husband's family, there is a history of twins. In fact, my father (the genealogist) informed me that twins existed all over the place when you looked back through our extended family of aunts and uncles. It's common knowledge that twins skip a generation. I looked at my own siblings, three brothers, no twins there. Bob is an only child, obviously no twins in his immediate direction. That left me with a double likelihood of having twins.

I'll tell you a secret about me. I've always wanted twins. Each and every time I became pregnant, I wished for twins. And furthermore, I always thought I'd have them. But after I had my second and third children I forgot about my fixation on twins.

When I found myself pregnant for the fourth time, twins were the furthest thing from my mind. In fact, having another child was the furthest thing from my mind! We had just moved into our white stucco home across the street from The Garden Villa. Nick was nearly eight and my youngest, Leslie, wasn't quite a year old. I literally ran two households, our retirement home on one side of the street and our busy family on the other. Then, out of the blue, I found myself on the receiving end of one of God's best surprises.

At first I didn't get it. I felt too sick. I awoke one morning and couldn't get out of bed which, for me, was unheard of. I did an inventory of my symptoms. I didn't feel like I had a fever, but I did feel lifeless. I diagnosed my condition as the flu. I pried myself off the mattress, got dressed, and tried to convince myself that I'd be better once I got moving. This time my "think positive" self-talk didn't help. After a week, I still didn't feel any better. That's when I learned that I wasn't "with flu," I was "with child"!

This being my fourth pregnancy, I was experienced in the ways of prenatal care and the rigors of childbirth. I was sure it wasn't necessary to get in touch right away with the midwife, Skippy King, who helped with Leslie's delivery. I took my prenatal vitamins and got as much rest as I could—which wasn't much, but I was used to that. I went on with my life and before I knew it, I was in my sixth month.

By then the size of my tummy stunned my midwife. I talked her out of her shocked reaction by reminding her that, after all, I had a history of large babies. I had been a large bundle of joy myself, when I bounded into the world weighing in at around ten pounds. Skippy calmed down and agreed to help me with my delivery, but she wanted to make sure everything was normal. She wanted me to get a sonogram.

The day I had that sonogram I learned my fantasy about having twins had come true. The doctor told me—and showed me—the two tiny creatures moving around inside me. On December 7, 1987, first Angel and a minute later, Aaron, made their entrances.

Nick was ecstatic to have a brother. Not that he didn't love his sisters to death, but it was great having a brother. Aaron and his twin sister, Angel, were delightful babies. As his mother, I will tell you right off the bat that Aaron, who is ten years old as of this writing, is a happy-go-lucky personality. I've raised him and I am here to tell you that he is a child who has never had a bad day! Nick is a more complex personality with a hidden, even moody side. The smiles on Aaron's face, which you see on tons of fan magazine pages, are genuine. His happiness is infectious!

Aaron grew up idolizing Nick. Everything his big brother did, Aaron wanted to do. He shadowed Nick, who was always very affectionate and playful and there for Aaron when it was time to learn how to swing a baseball bat or ride a skateboard. Nick taught Aaron how to do many things, some of which I wish Aaron hadn't learned! So it wasn't all that surprising to me that the big brother who showed the little one how to drink from a cup, or hurl a rock with a slingshot, would start showing his little brother how to hold a microphone.

Worlds Together and Worlds Apart

There is an eight-year age difference between Nick and Aaron. Nonetheless, they have so much in common, it's uncanny: blond locks, irrepressible energy, charisma, love of music, and the talent to sing and dance.

Their life experiences, though, have been very different. Aaron grew up as Nick's career kicked into high gear. He watched his brother perform, rehearse, and even tour. He also saw Nick go fishing and collect baseball cards. So to Aaron childhood consisted of both these worlds blurring the line between ordinary childhood and the extraordinary life of a child star. Show business was already sewn into the family fabric and schedule. Aaron watched BJ go along with Nick to photo shoots and on interviews for modeling assignments. It seemed perfectly normal to six-year-old Aaron to play with video games, ride his skateboard, fight with his twin sister, *and* model and perform. Watch the Backstreet Boys' home video, *Backstreet's Back Behind the Scenes,* and you'll see

Aaron in the background as the boys learn their choreography. It wasn't unusual for Fatima, the choreographer for the Backstreet Boys, to be running Nick and AJ and the rest of the group through their dance moves, while Aaron flipped and somersaulted in and out of the line.

All Bob and I did was point him in the right direction, enrolling Aaron in an after-school program of singing and playing music, a sort of "rock school." Aaron took the initiative to round up a few pint-sized musicians and join in as (what else?) the band's lead vocalist.

Aaron approaches performing differently than Nick did. Aaron watches and mimics everyone he sees, imitating a dance move here or a gesture there from a singer or dancer we've met on the road. These seem to meld until Aaron creates a style of his own. Nick, on the other hand, practiced alone, creating his style as he improved himself. The end result is the same. Both Nick and Aaron put on a great show.

Postcards from the Edge of Aaron's World Tour

Aaron is a younger version of Nick. A day in his life is a whirlwind.

Already an established pop sensation in his own right throughout Europe after best-selling singles like "Crush on You" and "Shake It," Aaron has appeal for audiences from Germany to Singapore. During the

German leg of Aaron's winter 1998 European tour he and I traveled to Berlin. As the bus pulled up to the hotel's front entrance, a throng of preadolescent blond frauleins jostled for position. The squeals pealed into the bus. Aaron peered out the window into the crowd. Meanwhile the bus driver's blood pressure rose because his job was to get us parked without running over zealous fans who mobbed buses that carried pop stars like mine.

We managed to get inside without any casualties. I steered Aaron through a crowd of giggling girls and up to our floor. As we made our way down the hallway toward our room, we saw scary Marilyn Manson and an entourage of straggly musicians standing in front of our door. Marilyn and his boys buzzed about the frenzy outside the hotel. They realized, to their dismay, that the girls below on the street weren't chanting "Marilyn! Marilyn!" The long hard road from hell just got a little harder for Marilyn. The girls below called out "Aaron! Aaron!" The rockers exchanged confused looks. They asked one another, "Who is Aaron?"

Aaron let their confusion dangle in the air but I couldn't resist and told them, "All the girls outside are here for my son, Aaron Carter." The entourage looked down at little Aaron, who, unfazed by the entire incident, flashed Marilyn and his boys a smile.

Here's another incident from the summer 1998 tour when Aaron was the opening act for the Backstreet Boys. After the show I watched and waited for Aaron to unwind. A knock sounded on the dressing room door. In walked Diana Ross with her young sons. The diva of soul herself came backstage to congratulate my younger son on his wonderful performance! We'd met Diana in Norway when our families stayed at the same hotel. At her invitation, Aaron played with her children, and Diana said she was impressed that Aaron was so "normal."

The stage mother battles I fought over the years on Nick's behalf I now fight for Aaron. I make sure he is allowed to be a child—to race in the park or gobble a submarine sandwich, or shop in a Kmart.

Bob and I detoured our tour bus to a local fair last July. Aaron rode on (and of course tried to rock) the ferris wheel. He nagged us to play arcade games. Aaron lives the life of a boy like any other who loves country fairs and hot dogs. Yet he takes the time to pose with girls who already know his name.

Double Trouble Teen Idol

Aaron confesses, "I wanted to become a pop star so I could spend more time with my brother."

Aaron asks and Nick gives advice. Art imitates life, sometimes, for these two brothers. Aaron's music video, "Crush on You," shows big brother Nick giving advice. Nick wrote the song "Ain't That Cute," telling Aaron to follow his dreams.

And Aaron tells fans about Nick's tips. One of Nick's gems of advice: "Behave when you are on the road." It seems this past summer, I was, on occasion, telling the two of them to do just that! They squabbled over the video game equipment!

Nick, who has grown mature and serious, is determined to help Aaron navigate fame and fortune. Nick and I agree on guidelines for Aaron, courtesy of our hindsight and mileage.

Aaron should not overwork to become a teen idol. Nick wants to make sure Aaron's schedule isn't all work and no play. So we keep Aaron to a strict four-hours-a-day rule. Promotions, rehearsals, vocal exercises, and performances cannot exceed that limit. The rest of the day is for school, fun, and family.

Aaron stays grounded. Nick says, "I'm here to watch over my baby brother. I've been through this and I intend to guide him. We're lucky today because there are shows on MTV and VH1 that tell the stories of the stars that have come before us. We get to watch what they went through in the past. You can use this for your own benefit. You don't sit back and say, 'That's not going to happen to me.' Instead you say that you've seen it happen before. You learn from it. This is a ruthless business. It can change a person. That's what I keep in mind for myself, and what I think of when I see my brother getting more and more successful. I tell Aaron that no matter how big he gets, I'm here to keep him grounded, even if that means knocking him down a few pegs."

Aaron gets tutored by a pro. Nick, Aaron, and I were backstage recently. Foreign record company promotional folks videotaped my twosome. Nick and Aaron wrestled with each other, just like they have always done. To me wrestling is really the way boys hug. When the camera rolled, Nick smiled and said, "I'm going to teach Aaron everything I know." What that means: double pleasure, double fun, and double teen idol fireworks.

A Final Curtain Call for Aaron

I sat in our living room playing Aaron's "Surfin USA" music video for a few friends. The music video shows Aaron on the beach, cutting up with the *Baywatch* beauties. While the VCR hums, my Aaron sings live for the benefit of those on my sofa.

Over in the corner, I left a stack of Nick's early costumes in a pile. I'd gotten those out to reminisce. Aaron dresses in Nick's old MC Hammer outfit, black velvet balloon pants and matching shirt, and looks like a whirling dervish spinning like a velveteen top. He brings that "Can't Touch This" memory right into center stage for me again. Aaron is set to do a TV sitcom. My sons plan to record some duets in the near future.

Here's one final peek into Aaron's life. It's five minutes to show time. He has run through his vocal exercises. He's centered himself. He's gotten into a shiny bright blue or red costume. Aaron, myself, the dancers, and Nick come together, joining hands for a prayer. Nick thanks God for their success, and asks Him to watch over the show, and all the fans in the audience. "May everyone stay safe," he murmurs. I reflect on my good fortune. At best, a mother is lucky enough to watch only one son reach for the stars and get there.

I feel Aaron's hand drop from my grasp. He gives me one last look. He grins at Nick. He bounds toward the stage and the roaring crowd greets him. "Hello, New York. I'm Aaron Carter."

Aaron started off as half of a set of twins, a dream come true for me. Now he is the stuff of dreams for a new generation of fans, and he's the pride and joy of his big brother.

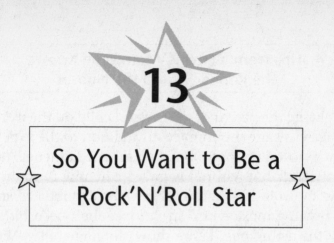

13

So You Want to Be a Rock'N'Roll Star

I've become a familiar face to the fans of my son. As Aaron continues to pursue his own brand of happy rock'n'roll music, his fans, too, are seeing me as part of the picture. I'm often asked for autographs, and—even more importantly—I'm asked for advice.

I want to say thank you to all the fans, first for believing in Nick's talent and for loving him. His great dream was to perform, and now, thanks to all his fans, that dream has come true. I'm getting ready to send my second wave of gratitude to Aaron's fans.

I have always wanted to help my children attain the kind of life that allows them to do whatever it is that makes each of them happy. For Nick—and Aaron, too—it is singing. But the music business can be treacherous.

Tips from a Loving Mom Who Knows the Ropes . . . and the Nooses

Being the parent of a successful child on the world stage gives me the courage, in addition to the experience, to talk about what I've seen. I launched not only Nick, but Aaron. My girls are itching to get into the showbiz action, too. BJ has already modeled and acted in a music video in Europe. She's been bitten by the acting bug. Leslie shows singing ability. Nick wants to work with her in the recording studio we've built in our home, maybe even produce her. Angel sings, but so far school interests her more than entertaining.

Whether you or your child wants to become a singer, musician, and dancer like Nick and Aaron, or break into modeling and acting like BJ, pay attention to these tips that Nick and I garnered on the way up. Learn how to be careful as well as calculating.

• *Get a second opinion on talent.* An artist has to believe in himself or herself, but sometimes people (even parents) overestimate the quality of a child's singing or dancing, or how photogenic a child is. Get that second appraisal, but try hard to judge objectively whether it's correct or exaggerated.

Teachers are a good source of second opinions. A drama teacher casting a child in a lead part, a chorus teacher giving a solo or a main singing part in a musical, a middle school play choreographer selecting a child to dance solo—getting singled out demonstrates that others recognize talent.

It's part of their job to motivate a child to practice that flute, or hit that high note on pitch. They may be less than honest about the merits of a performance.

People who get paid to help hone skills aren't always reliable. You cannot always trust the opinion of saxophone tutors, vocal instructors, or dance teachers because they are being paid to teach.

To do otherwise would be biting the hand that is paying their bills. So go beyond them.

Nick had Mrs. Daniels, Ms. Prinkey, and Sandy Karl singing his praises. I, of course, believed them when they told me how talented Nick was. However, I watched the faces in the audience at performances and at auditions to be sure.

• *Don't pay for anything. If you do, make certain you get something for your money.* The world of children's entertainment has more than a few con artists. Wherever there are unknowns with stardom in their eyes, there are charlatans who want to cash in on those folks and their innocent hopes. People tell aspiring youngsters that expensive portfolios of photographs are essential. Others insist on videotaping or recording the client, for a price, of course. Beware of the wolves in sheep's clothing who are out to fleece you.

It seemed that nearly everyone Nick came in contact with wanted a fee. Remember Nick's big television starring role? I had to pay for the acting time. The bottom line was, however, that Nick got acting, singing, recording, and filming experience. That was worth the expense.

I paid for Nick, but those kinds of experiences are out there for free. A child who wants to act, sing, or dance should look first in his or her own backyard at the many opportunities in local and regional community theater.

• *Get an agent as soon as possible.* A legitimate agent does not ask for money up front. A talent representative is also the best person to verify talent. An agent will only take on a client who will get the modeling assignment, the acting part, or the singing spot. Agents work on a commission, and that means they are paid when they get work for a singer, model, actor. No work, no earnings for them. Time is money, and no good agent will waste time on a child who doesn't have what it takes to succeed.

When I took Nick to audition for *The Clubhouse Kids* we went to a theater at the Tampa Performing Arts Center. There were at least fifty hopeful six- to twelve-year-olds and twice the number of parents accompanying them. We sat up in the seats. One by one the frightened children walked up on the stage and sang. Nick, also frightened, but determined and experienced from his work with June Daniels, blew everyone out of his seat with his voice. That day I met another mother, Peggy Obedzinski, who had two children, Shane and Audra, with talent and dreams. She volunteered to teach me what I needed to know about breaking in.

Peggy recommended the best local agents and

told me to sign up with a few of them as opposed to signing an exclusive deal with one. Nick and I probably couldn't have gotten away with this in Los Angeles or New York City, but this was Tampa.

Peggy's shrewd tip worked out well enough at first. Then the agents found out that Nick wasn't just a pretty face with an animated personality—he could sing. As Nick began getting hotter, several agents called us all at once for an upcoming opportunity. I used to take the first call and get all the details and tell the agent Nick would be there. Then I'd tell Nick and Bob, "Don't answer the telephone. It's only going to be one of the other agents calling."

Peggy shared so much insider information with me—like how to write up a resume for Nick, highlighting his hobbies and his credits. She also taught us "to slate." At auditions, a real professional "slates," meaning he announces his name, age, and the agent who represents him. So, learn to network. It's always a good strategy.

• *Get photographs.* Nick and I went to a local photographer, J. P. Turnball, well known at the time in Tampa acting circles. We came away with great pictures and even greater free advice. J. P. told us that a good picture is necessary, even though he whispered that nine out of ten people who do the auditioning don't even bother looking at them. Too many parents go overboard. They hire a photographer to take lots of pictures in a variety of settings, indoors and outdoors, with their child in casual and formal poses and all decked out. A whole portfolio is not something the average parent can afford. Nor is it a must—because preadolescents hit growth spurts and look totally different every six months. Just look at Nick's photographs at twelve and thirteen.

- *The best talent looks natural.* I got this advice from talent agents and photographers, but I didn't understand it at first. When Nick got ready for those initial modeling screenings or acting jobs, he dressed in his best clothes. I'd nag Nick to let me comb his hair until not a strand was out of place.

I began to notice that waiting rooms at auditions were full of perfectly coifed and clothed girls and boys, but they weren't the ones who triumphed. It was the underdressed, ordinary child who usually got the part. When Nick and I went out to Los Angeles to audition once, children dressed even more casually—torn jeans, sandals, messy hair.

What advertising executives and television producers want is a child who looks natural. Real-looking children are most convincing. I took Aaron to an agent who handled Nick. She snapped Aaron up. She sent us to try for a print ad for a housing development. The planned shot was to capture a boy fishing off the dock with a grandfatherly type. Tons of perfectly adorable boys came; Aaron was chosen.

The person in charge told me afterward, "Do you know why Aaron got the shot? He looked like a real little boy. We loved the scars on his face." Aaron has two scars, one from when he fell on our family boat. The other scar on his lip came from a dog bite. We once took in an older dog who wasn't used to children. Out in the yard one day, Aaron roughhoused;

the dog lashed out. We had to give that dog away after that.

With Nick I learned by trial and error. By the time I took Aaron on the rounds, I knew the ins and outs. Always be yourself; that's the only true star ingredient, and the best.

• *Know your limitations.* I've told you that an aspiring child who is a triple threat has the best odds. A singing, dancing, personality-plus acting youngster goes after a wider variety of opportunities. More tries equals better luck.

That doesn't mean a child has to master the three. A child who can't sing or who doesn't have the right look for modeling cannot be magically transformed. If you are just a singer or just an actor, that will be enough. Look at Frank Sinatra. He sang and acted but he was not a great dancer. Not being a triple-threat performer didn't hurt his career.

Sometimes you can develop a skill. Believe it or not, Nick had two left feet when he started. Now when you watch him dance to his music, he's a dance machine. Both child star dreamers and parents have to learn to gauge talent, expectations, and limitations. It is a tricky balancing act.

• *Keep your star search in perspective.* Wanting to become a model, a Spice Girl, or the next singing sensation has to be more than a fantasy. Yet it cannot be the only thing, or most important thing in a person's life. At times it is hard for a child to keep this in perspective. A child must never be allowed to measure his worth by the outcome of an audition or the verdict of a casting director.

The best way to look at trying to become an entertainer or model is to think of it as a journey in which you discover who you are and where you want to go. I always praised Nick when he triumphed and dismissed the importance of a job or a part when he got passed over. I'd tell him, "You are a great kid, no matter what" or "Don't worry about it, because there will be other chances in the future." I never let Nick's self-esteem or self-image be determined by show business. He was a singer, model, dancer, actor—yes. But what really counted to me was the way Nick performed as a son, a big brother, a student, a citizen, and a helping hand around our elderly residents. This emphasis on character and compassion, on the spiritual side of life and not the material side, on what's inside a person and not what others think—these messages proved to be the most important guidance I gave Nick.

Nick Carter is a big star now. Yet, Nick separates the roar of the crowd, the luster of fame, and even the perks of fortune from the important core of who he is.

When Nick comes home from the Backstreet world, he reverts back to being an ordinary teenager. Nick gets in his green Durango truck and heads for the mall, takes his boat out, or hangs with friends. I'll let Nick explain.

"When I come home, I don't think about business. I really don't even think about singing at all. I will sit down and write songs because that's something I enjoy doing. I'm writing for Aaron's next album right now. When I'm here in Florida, I'm oblivious to the whole business. I try not to think about working because this is my time to be normal. If you can come back home, and be who you are underneath all the star stuff, that's what's important.

"Some people would come home and use what they are doing, their position as a celebrity, to take advantage of people, say to get girlfriends or whatever. I don't do that. I don't want to talk about that side of me here at home. People who know me know that I don't want to be treated like anyone other than me, Normal Nick."

It's hard to imagine but people who know the quieter, unglamorous side like that part of Nick even more than the hot pop singer, the cool teen idol. I love both sides.

It's funny, but as I write out these lessons for stardom, it occurs to me that many of them have value for life in general. It's all about finding balance and finding trustworthy relationships, being true to yourself and knowing what really counts. The bottom line is that you have to make your own luck, as they say, with smart calculating and careful planning—*and* keeping yourself on track. Staying grounded is fundamental. Reaching for the stars can make you lose your footing. Looking up all the time can make you oblivious to the joy of things all around you. It can burn you unless you are tethered firmly to the earth and to the people who love you.

This advice is geared toward aspiring entertainers, but it is worthwhile for anyone. Whether it's sports, the sciences, the arts, building houses, or planting rose gardens—the same rules apply.

☆ Nick Gets the Last Word ☆

I wanted to tell here about Nick's life up until he became a Backstreet Boy . . . to communicate how hard Nick worked to develop the talent that seemed to go into overdrive once he collaborated with Brian Littrel, Kevin Richardson, A. J. McLean, and Howie Dorough. I hope I've accomplished those goals.

What was the moment like for Nick when he "made it"? How did success feel? Along the way there were many times when Nick was proud—winning a prize at a talent showcase, proving himself at an audition—yet how did he react to touching the star he so often wished upon? I'll let him have the last word.

Nick Becomes a Backstreet "Boy Wonder"

"My mom and I were very happy the day I signed with Jive as one of the Backstreet Boys. I was fifteen years old. Signing on the dotted line of a recording contract is something that many people dream of, and doing so at only fifteen was an accomplishment in itself.

"We didn't celebrate at first, because we'd been disappointed a lot of times when people made promises, made deals—then nothing happened! So when this Jive deal went through, I had a little hesitation. My mom, as she had always done before, told me to prepare myself for *anything*—the code word for good or bad news."

Yes, Nick and I held our breath that day. It took a while before we could realize the golden opportunities. Then came heady days with and for the Backstreet Boys.

That fraternity of rock-stars-in-training and the grueling apprenticeship they served is another book in itself. I had driven the car up until that point. Next Nick was on a Backstreet Boys bus, and his father was driving it. If you want to know what happened then, maybe we can talk Bob into picking up where I am leaving off here.

Those years make up another diary full of secrets about Nick Carter, his heart and soul. . . .

Are You a Real Nick-o-Phile?

Now that you have come to the end of *The Heart and Soul of Nick Carter: Secrets Only a Mother Knows,* are you ready to test yourself? Maybe if you get a good grade, Nick will congratulate you. This gives you an opportunity to prove to yourself, your parents, and your teachers, that you do, indeed, have super-reading comprehension!

Directions: This is a multiple choice test. Read each of the statements or questions. Then choose the correct answer. Put your choice in the space provided. Proceed to the Scoring Section. Fill in your answer and next to it give yourself the points you deserve by looking at the table that is provided. Total your score. Read your evaluation.

1. What celebrity model autographed her famous face with "Happy Birthday, Nick"? **(a)** Tyra Banks; **(b)** Kate Moss; **(c)** Cindy Crawford; **(d)** Jennifer Lopez   1. ___

2. The pet iguana that lives at Nick's Florida home is named **(a)** Garfunkel; **(b)** Baby Face; **(d)** Puff Daddy; **(d)** Fric.

2. ____

3. Who spent the most time teaching Nick to write his A B Cs? **(a)** his mom; **(b)** Helen, his residential grandmother; **(c)** Grandfather Douglas; **(d)** his dad

3. ____

4. The Yankee Rebel was chosen as the name for the Carter's first nightclub because **(a)** Nick's grandparents—a rebel from Tennessee and a Yankee—lent the money to start it up; **(b)** it reminded Jane of the Yankee Clipper and her *Mayflower* heritage; **(c)** Jane and Bob felt like young renegades; **(d)** they saw the name scrawled in the bathroom.

4. ____

5. What was the very first song that Nick sang for an audience? **(a)** "Go Fly a Kite"; **(b)** "Bridge Over Troubled Water"; **(c)** "Supercalifragilisticexpialidocious"; **(d)** "You Ain't Nothing but a Hound Dog"

5. ____

6. What famous rock'n'roll star did Nick *never* dress up like and build a song around? **(a)** Elvis Presley; **(b)** Elton John; **(c)** M.C. Hammer; **(d)** Paul McCartney

6. ____

7. Nick wore all of the following costumes on Holloween except for one. Which is it? **(a)** Count Dracula; **(b)** Freddy Krueger; **(c)** The Wolf Man; **(d)** Casper the Ghost

7. ____

8. During which famous American military battle did Carter ancestors prominently fight and die? **(a)** The War of 1812; **(b)** The Civil War; **(c)** The Battle of Bunker Hill; **(d)** The storming of Iwo Jima

8. ____

9. What kind of dog stood guard—*slept* guard—right next to Nick when he lived like a gypsy, napping under the open sky by day and sleeping in a van under the stars at night? **(a)** A Doberman pinscher; **(b)** a Samoyed; **(c)** a golden retriever; **(d)** a French poodle

9. ____

10. What was Nick's sister BJ's reaction to the news that Nick and the rest of the family were moving out of Tampa into a huge house on the water? **(a)** BJ jumped for joy and hugged her big brother; **(b)** BJ hid under the bed in protest because she didn't want to move at all; **(c)** BJ went from room to room and started packing the belongings of everyone in cardboard boxes; **(d)** BJ went down to the kitchen and baked a chocolate cake to celebrate, nearly burning down the house in the process. 10. ____

11. With which of the following does Nick love to satisfy his sweet tooth? **(a)** peanut butter and jelly sandwiches at midnight; **(b)** Swiss Miss cocoa; **(c)** Swiss cake rolls; **(d)** Tootsie Rolls 11. ____

12. When Nick was a child in the Florida family residential home, he was befriended by **(a)** a wildlife artist who sketched cardinals; **(b)** an old man who collected butterflies; **(c)** an elderly woman who made jewelry with acorns; **(d)** a man who carved birds with a Swiss Army knife. 12. ____

13. Nick has shown that he's a regular trouper by putting on a show in this most unlikely locale—**(a)** a cow pasture; **(b)** a platform out in the Arizona desert; **(c)** acting like a fool on a hill; **(d)** performing in a circus. 13. ____

14. What notorious rock'n'roll rockstar/shockstar did Aaron bump into over in Europe? **(a)** Howard Stern; **(b)** Marilyn Manson; **(c)** Courtney Love; **(d)** Madonna 14. ____

15. What sport can you find Nick playing in the hours before a concert performance backstage or underneath the stage? **(a)** volleyball; **(b)** football; **(c)** basketball; **(d)** Lacrosse 15. ____

16. Can you name the two cities that Nick traveled back and forth between so often the tires on his mom's car showed signs of wear and tear? **(a)** Tampa and Orlando; **(b)** Miami and St. Petersburg; **(c)** Tampa and Clearwater; **(d)** St. Augustine and Daytona Beach 16. ____

17. In Nick's bedroom he keeps a prized collection of all but one of the following—**(a)** hats; **(b)** stuffed animals; **(c)** baseball cards; **(d)** stamps from fan mail around the world. 17. ____

18. During his early years, Nick had leading parts in stage performances that had these animals written into the scripts: **(a)** a rooster and a chick; **(b)** a wolf and a turkey; **(c)** a dog and a spider; **(d)** an alley cat and a hound. 18. ____

19. What was the low point according to Nick about his middle school life? **(a)** He broke his arm in the middle school cafeteria; **(b)** He felt excluded and uncomfortable around peers who didn't understand him; **(c)** He got into a feud over a girl with the town bully; **(d)** He fell asleep in class and was sent down to the assistant principal's office.   **19.** ___

20. All but one of the following famous sayings mean a lot to Nick and have figured in his upbringing: **(a)** Honesty is the best policy; **(b)** Beauty is only skin deep; **(c)** If at first you don't succeed, try again; **(d)** Sometimes nice guys finish last.   **20.** ___

Scoring: Here are a listing of the correct answers. For every correct answer give yourself 5 points.

YOUR ANSWERS	CORRECT ANSWERS	POINTS	YOUR ANSWERS	CORRECT ANSWERS	POINTS
1.	c	_____	11.	c	_____
2.	b	_____	12.	d	_____
3.	b	_____	13.	a	_____
4.	a	_____	14.	b	_____
5.	b	_____	15.	c	_____
6.	d	_____	16.	a	_____
7.	c	_____	17.	d	_____
8.	c	_____	18.	b	_____
9.	a	_____	19.	b	_____
10.	b	_____	20.	a	_____

Evaluation:

0 to 35 Points: *Roll with It!*

If you scored in this low range, and you are feeling badly about it, put on Nick's vocal of "Roll with It" and sing it ten times. I promise you will feel better. Then reread Nick's biography, *The Heart and Soul of Nick Carter: Secrets Only a Mother Knows,* and see where you made your mistakes. Maybe you were just too distracted by all the glossy pictures of Nick and you couldn't concentrate. Don't give up. Do what Nick does when life gets him down, just roll with it.

40 to 65 Points: *As Long as You Love Me!*

If you scored in this middle range, you better go back and check the facts a bit more closely in Nick's biography of his early years, *The Heart and Soul of Nick Carter: Secrets Only a Mother Knows.* You knew some of the facts but got mixed up because some of the questions were tricky. For example, Nick's first public performance was with a rendition of "Go Fly a Kite," but the very first song he sang for an audience of one, me, was "Bridge Over Troubled Water." Don't be too hard on yourself. As long as you love Nick enough to try, he won't hold a low score against you.

70 to 100 Points: *Rock Your Body!*

Everybody who scores in this—the highest range—gets to rock your body! You have wonderful reading comprehension skills. Despite some trick questions designed just to stump you, you showed that you are sharp enough to select the correct answer anyway. You know your *Peter and the Wolf* and your *Griswald the Turkey* trivia. You are an official recognized Nick-O-Phile. On behalf of my son, Nick, I thank you for your attention to the details of his biography. You don't have to reread *The Heart and Soul of Nick Carter: Secrets Only a Mother Knows,* but I hope you will.

No matter how you scored, Nick says everyone gets an A for effort!